Tea at the Palace

Tea at the Palace

A COOKBOOK

CAROLYN ROBB

PHOTOGRAPHS BY JOHN KERNICK

weldon**owen**

Contents

–Carolyn Robb
Oxfordshire 2021

For Mandy, because no one loves making and
eating beautiful cakes more than you do.

Introduction

During my thirteen years as a royal chef, I was very privileged to call some of Britain's most splendid royal palaces and castles my "place of work." It was immensely inspiring to cook for such incredible people in such impressive surroundings. Each royal residence has its own distinctive character, traditions, and ambience, dictated by its whereabouts and its history, which, in many cases, dates back hundreds of years. I have created this collection of special recipes in celebration of a unique aspect of each of the twelve superb locations.

The grandeur of Windsor Castle contrasts wonderfully with the quirkiness of the Brighton Pavilion, the tranquillity of Highgrove, the rustic Scottish charm of The Castle of Mey, and the dollhouse perfection of Kew Palace. The splendor of Blenheim Palace and majesty of Buckingham Palace are worlds away from the country-house charm of Sandringham. Henry VIII's beloved Hampton Court, Queen Victoria's peaceful Highlands' retreat of Balmoral Castle, and the imposing medieval Welsh waterside fortress of Caernarfon Castle all have evocative tales of bygone times to tell. The chapter devoted to Kensington Palace is bursting with whimsicality. I was very lucky to call "KP" my home during the time that I cooked for TRH The Duke and Duchess of Gloucester and TRH The Prince and Princess of Wales, Prince William, and Prince Harry.

Within these pages, there is an afternoon tea for every taste, whether that be elegant or rustic, summery or warming, savory or chocolatey, fanciful or flowery, or quite simply regal. As Henry James said, "There are few hours in life more agreeable than the hour dedicated to the ceremony of afternoon tea."

Happy Cooking!

Carolyn Robb

Buckingham Palace

Summer Garden Parties

London is home to eleven royal palaces. Buckingham Palace, the Queen's official London residence, is by far the best known. Each year, hundreds of thousands of tourists flock to the palace to peer through the famous black-and-gold railings in the hope of catching a glimpse of the Queen. At times, it is a gathering place for national celebration, such as royal weddings and jubilees and the annual Trooping the Colour parade in celebration of Her Majesty's birthday. For all of these occasions, the royal family stands on the famous balcony on the front façade of the palace to greet the legions of well-wishers. On May 8, 1945, huge crowds gathered at Buckingham Palace to celebrate VE (Victory in Europe) Day, and the family made an unprecedented eight balcony appearances that day!

The palace's best-kept secret is the extraordinary forty-two-acre (seventeen-hectare) private garden behind the building. From outside the railings, there is no clue that this beautiful and extensive green space even exists. It is here, in this wonderfully secluded oasis in the heart of London, that every spring and summer the Queen hosts three garden parties. Each of the events is attended by an incredible eight thousand guests. One couldn't hope to be part of a more patriotic celebration. These garden parties capture the spirit of everything that is British, with cream scones, mighty jugs of

Pimm's, a brass band playing Edward Elgar's "Land of Hope and Glory," and dapper gentlemen in top hats and tails all part of the majestic scene!

The recipes in this chapter are representative of what is served to Her Majesty's guests at these remarkable garden parties. They are simple, seasonal, colorful, and quintessentially British. Each one of them would surely get the royal seal of approval.

Personal garden party invitation from the Lord Chamberlain.

Tangerine and Passion Fruit Melting Moments

"Melting moments" (see photograph on page 14) have a royal pedigree. I made them for a royal christening tea, and they were served at several of the annual palace garden parties I attended. Traditionally, these buttery, melt-in-one's-mouth cookies have a vanilla filling. However, by adding a generous amount of freshly grated tangerine zest and some wonderfully tangy fresh passion fruit, they are elevated to another level of delight. Don't be put off making these because of the need to pipe them, as the dough can just as successfully be rolled into balls by hand, flattened between the palms, and finished by pressing down with the tines of a fork.

FOR THE BISCUITS

1 cup plus 2 tablespoons (255 g) butter, at room temperature

⅔ cup (80 g) confectioners' sugar

½ teaspoon pure vanilla extract

2 tangerines

2 cups (250 g) cake flour

¾ cup (80 g) custard powder (see Chef's Note)

FOR THE BUTTERCREAM

6 tablespoons (80 g) butter, at room temperature

1⅓ cups (160 g) sifted confectioners' sugar

½ teaspoon pure vanilla extract

2 tablespoons passion fruit juice, from pulp of 1 large passion fruit rubbed through a sieve

Confectioners' sugar, for dusting

MAKES 20 SANDWICH BISCUITS

To make the biscuits, preheat the oven to 350°F (180°C). Line 2 sheet pans with parchment paper or silicone mats.

In a large bowl, using an electric mixer, beat together the butter and sugar on medium speed until light and creamy. Add the vanilla and beat until incorporated. Finely grate the zest from both tangerines directly into the bowl, then sift together the flour and custard powder directly into the bowl. Using a wooden spoon, mix to form a smooth dough that is soft enough to be piped.

Spoon the dough into a piping bag fitted with a ½-inch (12-mm) closed star tip. Then, moving in a tight counter-clockwise circle to shape each biscuit, pipe rosettes about 1½ inches (4 cm) in diameter onto the prepared pans, spacing them about 1 inch (2.5 cm) apart. You should have 40 biscuits total.

Bake the biscuits until lightly golden, 10–12 minutes. Let cool on the pans on wire racks for a few minutes, then transfer to the racks to cool completely.

While the biscuits are baking, make the buttercream. In a bowl, using the electric mixer, beat the butter on high speed until lightened and smooth, about 1 minute. Add the sugar, vanilla, and passion fruit juice and beat for several minutes until the mixture is very light and creamy.

Spoon the buttercream into a piping bag fitted with a ¼-inch (6-mm) plain tip. Turn half of the biscuits bottom side up on a work surface. Pipe a generous amount of the buttercream onto each of the overturned biscuits. Then place a second biscuit, bottom side down, on top of the buttercream, pressing gently to secure in place.

Lightly dust the tops with sugar. The sandwich biscuits will keep in an airtight container at room temperature for up to 5 days.

 CHEF'S NOTE

You can vary the flavor of both the biscuits and the buttercream. Among my favorite combinations are chocolate-mint, chocolate-orange, chocolate-vanilla, and chocolate-raspberry. Each is made by replacing the tangerine zest with 2 tablespoons unsweetened cocoa powder and replacing the passion fruit juice with a few drops of peppermint, orange, pure vanilla, or raspberry extract. If opting for peppermint-, orange-, and raspberry-flavored buttercream, tint with the appropriate natural food coloring. If you cannot find fresh passion fruit, use store-bought passion fruit juice, checking the label to be sure it is 100 percent juice with no sugar added. Look for custard powder in specialty food shops or online (Bird's is the most popular UK brand). If you are unable to purchase it, substitute an equal amount of cornstarch.

Little Scones with Raspberries and Clotted Cream

*T*here is an age-old debate among connoisseurs of the cream tea—afternoon tea consisting of tea served with scones, clotted cream, and jam—as to whether the cream or the jam goes on top. In the West Country where cream teas originated, Devon and Cornwall are neighboring counties. Traditionally, a Devon cream tea has the cream sitting on the scone, then the jam on top of the cream, while a Cornish cream tea has the jam as the first ingredient on the scone, followed by the cream, so this argument is unlikely ever to be settled! These bite-size scones (see photograph on page 15) are always popular, especially with children. You can substitute strawberry jam and strawberries for the raspberry jam and raspberries.

FOR THE SCONES

3⅔ cups (450 g) cake flour

4 teaspoons baking powder

¼ cup (50 g) superfine sugar

Pinch of salt

7 tablespoons (100 g) butter, at room temperature, cut into cubes

2 free-range eggs

About ¾ cup (180 ml) whole milk

TO SERVE

Raspberry jam

¾ cup (200 ml) clotted cream (see Chef's Note)

Confectioners' sugar, for dusting

Raspberries

Tiny fresh mint sprigs (optional)

MAKES 36 MINI SCONES

Preheat the oven to 425°F (220°C). Line a large sheet pan with parchment paper or a silicone mat.

Sift together the flour, baking powder, sugar, and salt into a large bowl. Scatter the butter over the flour mixture and, using your fingertips, rub the butter into the dry ingredients just until the mixture has the consistency of fine bread crumbs.

Break the eggs into a measuring pitcher and add milk as needed to total 1¼ cups (300 ml) liquid. Whisk together with a fork. Make a well in the center of the dry ingredients and add most of the liquid to the well, keeping a little of it back in case you don't need all of it. Using a round-bladed table knife, mix together the egg mixture and the flour mixture to achieve a lightly bound dough that is neither sticky nor dry and crumbly, adding more of the liquid if needed. Do not overmix.

Turn the dough out onto a lightly floured work surface and, working quickly, knead the dough very lightly to rid it of any cracks. Pat the dough out to a thickness of ¾ inch (2 cm). Using a 1½-inch (4-cm) plain round cutter, cut out as many rounds as possible, dipping the cutter into flour before each cut to ensure a clean cut. Transfer the cutouts to the prepared pan, spacing them about 1 inch (2.5 cm) apart. Gather up the scraps, press together, pat out, cut out more rounds, and add to the pan.

Bake the scones until well risen and golden, 8–10 minutes. Transfer to a wire rack to cool.

To serve, split the scones horizontally and top each half with jam and a dollop of cream. Dust very lightly with confectioners' sugar and accompany with a bowl of raspberries. Garnish with mint, if desired.

♔ CHEF'S NOTE

In the West Country, clotted cream is traditionally made by heating unpasteurized milk until a thick layer of cream settles on top, which is then lifted off once the milk cools. Exports from the area are made from pasteurized milk and are available in specialty markets and online.

Strawberry Bunting Cake

The classic Victoria sandwich cake is the centerpiece of every garden party afternoon tea spread. There is no cake more regal than this! It was originally made for Queen Victoria, during whose incredible sixty-six-year reign the tradition of afternoon tea began to evolve. It is remarkable that despite how much the world has changed during the sixty-nine-year reign of Queen Elizabeth II, the tradition of afternoon tea is ever more popular. Queen Victoria would have had her cake sandwiched together with raspberry jam and topped with a sprinkling of granulated sugar. I have filled this cake with strawberry jam, whipped cream, and fresh berries, topped it with more berries and a few fresh rose petals, and then added some celebratory mini Union Jack bunting! It is a cake befitting Queen Elizabeth II, who is already the longest-reigning monarch in British history and who will, in 2022, celebrate her Platinum Jubilee: seventy amazing years on the throne.

FOR THE CAKE

1 cup (225 g) unsalted butter, at room temperature, plus more for the pans

1 cup plus 2 tablespoons (225 g) superfine sugar

1 teaspoon pure vanilla extract

4 free-range eggs

1¾ cups (225 g) cake flour

1 tablespoon baking powder

1 tablespoon boiling water

FOR THE FILLING

6 tablespoons (110 g) strawberry jam

¾ cup (180 ml) heavy cream, whipped

12 large strawberries, stemmed and sliced

Preheat the oven to 350°F (180°C). Butter the sides of two 8-inch (20-cm) round cake pans and line the bottom of each pan with parchment paper.

In a large bowl, using an electric mixer, beat together the butter and sugar on medium speed until creamy and light in color. Add the vanilla and then the eggs, one at a time, beating well after each addition. If the mixture starts to curdle, add a few spoons of the flour. Sift together the (remaining) flour and baking powder into the butter mixture and, using a large metal spoon or a rubber spatula, mix carefully just until all the flour mixture is evenly incorporated. Lastly, stir in the boiling water.

Divide the batter evenly between the prepared pans. Using an offset spatula, smooth the surface of the batter in each pan, then make a small hollow in the center so the top is flat when the cake layer emerges from the oven.

Recipe continues on the following page

Continued from the previous page

FOR THE DECORATION

12 medium strawberries

Handful of fresh rose petals

Confectioners' sugar, for dusting

Mini bunting about 12 inches (30 cm) long, 2 red-and-white paper drinking straws, and 2 thin wooden skewers

Serves 8–10

Bake the cake layers until the tops are golden and spring back to the touch and a toothpick inserted into the center of each cake comes out clean, 20–25 minutes. Let cool in the pans on wire racks for 10 minutes, then invert the pans onto the racks, lift off the pans, turn the layers right side up, and let cool completely.

To assemble and decorate the cake, trim the tops of the cake layers so they will sit flat, if necessary. Place a cake layer, top side down, on a serving plate. Spoon on the jam and spread gently to the edges. Top with the cream, again spreading gently to the edges, and finish with the strawberry slices, covering the cream evenly. Top with the second cake layer, top side up. Arrange the strawberries around the top edge of the cake, fill the center with the rose petals, and then dust lightly with confectioners' sugar. Secure each end of the bunting to the top of a straw-encased skewer and then pierce the skewers into either side of the base of the cake.

Nectarine and Red Currant Meringue Crowns

*T*hese simple, crisp meringues (see photograph on page 14) add a lovely splash of color to any afternoon tea spread. The tangy crème fraîche cuts through the sweetness of the meringues, while the nectarines and red currants are bursting with the flavors of the English summer.

FOR THE MERINGUE

3 free-range egg whites, at room temperature

Pinch of salt

¾ cup (150 g) superfine sugar

FOR THE TOPPING

1 ¼ cups (280 g) crème fraîche

2 nectarines, pitted and cut into small slices

2 sprigs fresh red currants

20 tiny fresh mint sprigs (optional)

Confectioners' sugar, for dusting

MAKES 20 CROWNS

 CHEF'S NOTE

Serve the crowns within a couple of hours of assembly, as the meringue will soften once the crowns are filled. Unfilled crowns will keep in an airtight container at room temperature for up to 10 days.

To make the meringue, preheat the oven to 190°F (90°C). Line 2 sheet pans with parchment paper or silicone mats.

In a large bowl, using an electric mixer, beat the egg whites on medium speed until they double in volume and hold a soft peak when the beaters are lifted. With the mixer running on medium speed, add the salt and then add the sugar, a tablespoon at a time, incorporating each addition completely before adding the next spoonful. Continue beating until all the sugar has been added, then set the mixer to high speed and beat until the meringue is light and very glossy.

Spoon the meringue into a piping bag fitted with a ¼-inch (6-mm) plain tip. Set a 2-inch (5-cm) plain round cutter in the corner of a prepared pan. Using the cutter as a guide, and starting in the center, pipe a base inside the cutter, then carefully lift off the cutter. Repeat to make 20 bases total. Then pipe a single row of dots around the edge of each base to form a crown.

Bake the meringues until they are crisp and lift off the paper or mat easily, about 2 hours. Let cool completely on the pans on wire racks. Transfer the crowns to a large tray. Place about a tablespoon of crème fraîche in the center of each crown. Top with a little nectarine, a sprig of red currants, and a mint sprig, if desired. Dust with confectioners' sugar just before serving.

Sandringham House

Autumn Shooting Party Tea

Located in Norfolk in East Anglia, Sandringham is a much-loved country retreat of the Queen and has been the private home of four generations of British monarchs. Just before he died in 1861, Queen Victoria's husband, Prince Albert, who had been searching for a country house for his eldest son, Edward, found what he wanted. He failed to complete the purchase before his death, but Edward concluded it the following year. Then, in 1870, Edward demolished the house and built a grand Jacobethan-style home characterized by wonderful gables and turrets. In the years since then, additions have been made, most notably the ballroom.

George V established the custom of spending Christmas at Sandringham, one which the family continues today. On December 25, 1932, George VI made the first Christmas broadcast on live radio from the "business room" at Sandringham, and twenty-five years later, Queen Elizabeth made the first live televised Christmas message from the library. The Queen's Christmas speech, always broadcast at three o'clock on Christmas Day, is watched by millions every year, as they pause their festivities for a few minutes to hear her sage words.

I traveled to Sandringham twice a year with Prince Charles, once in the spring and then in the autumn. The autumn visit was during the shooting season, when guests would enjoy long days out in the fields. Norfolk in November is one of the coldest, grayest, dampest places on earth, so guests needed more than the traditional dainty afternoon tea fare to sustain them! For this reason, I always served a hearty spread of autumnal teatime treats made from such wonderful local ingredients as wildflower honey, apples from the Sandringham orchards, and blackberries picked in the estate's hedgerows. I have woven a thread of warming spices through all of these recipes.

Glazed Apple and Pecan Cake

Bursting with the flavors of autumn, this is a lovely alternative to a traditional fruit cake, and the chunks of fresh apple make it deliciously moist. It is topped with a glistening apricot glaze, which lends a festive appearance. The orchards at Sandringham are the source of the most beautiful apples. My favorite variety was Howgate Wonder—gorgeous, huge, sweet, juicy cooking apples.

¾ cup (170 g) butter, melted and cooled, plus more for the pan

2¾ cups (340 g) cake flour, plus more for the pan

3 range-free eggs

1 cup (150 g) loosely packed light muscovado sugar

4 teaspoons baking powder

2 teaspoons ground cinnamon

3 medium apples, such as Howgate Wonder, Cox's Orange Pippin, Honeycrisp, or Braeburn

¾ cup (100 g) soft pitted dates, roughly chopped

½ cup (50 g) pecan halves, roughly chopped

6 tablespoons (110 g) apricot jam

SERVES 12

Preheat the oven to 350°F (180°C). Butter the bottom and sides of an 8-inch (20-cm) round springform pan, then dust the sides with flour, tapping out the excess, and line the bottom with parchment paper.

In a medium bowl, lightly whisk the eggs, then whisk in the butter until well blended. In a large bowl, stir together the flour, sugar, baking powder, and cinnamon until all the ingredients are evenly distributed.

Core 2 of the apples and cut them into ½-inch (12-mm) cubes, leaving the skin on. Stir the cubed apples, dates, and half of the pecans into the flour mixture, coating them evenly. Then pour the butter mixture into the flour mixture and gently stir together, making sure no small pockets of flour mixture remain.

Spoon the batter into the prepared pan and smooth the top with an offset spatula. Slice the remaining unpeeled apple crosswise into paper-thin circles and discard the seeds. Arrange the slices over the top of the cake and then sprinkle with the remaining pecans.

Bake the cake until a toothpick inserted into the center comes out clean, 50–60 minutes. As the cake bakes, the apple slices will curl at the edges. After about 40 minutes, loosely cover the top of the cake with a piece of aluminum foil to prevent the apple slices from burning.

Let cool in the pan on a wire rack for 10 minutes, then unclasp the pan sides and lift them off. Invert the cake onto a second wire rack and remove the base of the pan and parchment paper from the bottom of the cake. Turn the cake right side up. While the cake is still warm, in a small saucepan, heat the jam over low heat. Brush the warm jam over the top and sides of the cake, then let the cake cool completely before serving.

Gingerbread Bakewell Tartlets

*T*he Bakewell tart originated in the market town of Bakewell, nestled in the beautiful Derbyshire Dales. My twist on the classic recipe gives it a distinctly warming feel, perfect for cheering up a gloomy autumn afternoon. The lightly spiced pastry shell is filled with chunky apricot jam and topped with a rich gingerbread frangipane. Served fresh from the oven, still warm and perhaps with a dollop of whipped cream, these tarts are the ultimate afternoon-tea comfort food, especially at the end of a long, cold day outdoors.

FOR THE SPICED PASTRY

½ cup plus 2 tablespoons (140 g) chilled butter, diced

¼ cup plus 2 tablespoons (70 g) superfine sugar

1 free-range egg yolk

½ teaspoon pure vanilla extract

1¾ cups (225 g) cake flour

½ teaspoon ground ginger

½ teaspoon mixed spice (see Chef's Note, page 38)

FOR THE FILLING

3 ½ tablespoons (50 g) butter, at room temperature

¼ cup (50 g) superfine sugar

1 free-range egg

½ cup plus 1 tablespoon (50 g) ground almonds

2 tablespoons cake flour

1 teaspoon ground ginger

1 teaspoon mixed spice

2 tablespoons black treacle or honey

¾ cup (200 g) chunky apricot jam

3 tablespoons ginger syrup, from a jar of stem ginger

MAKES 12 TARTLETS

Preheat the oven to 425°F (220°C). Cut 12 strips of parchment paper each 1 inch (2.5 cm) wide and 6 inches (15 cm) long. Place a strip in each of the 12 cups of a standard muffin pan, extending the ends over the cup rim. The parchment makes it easier to remove the tartlets from the pan once they are baked.

To make the pastry, in a food processor, combine the butter and sugar and process just until combined. Add the egg yolk and vanilla and then the flour, ginger, and mixed spice. Pulse until the dough starts to come together, then turn the dough out onto a lightly floured work surface and finish bringing it together by hand. Gently shape into a smooth disk.

Roll out the dough no more than ¼ inch (6 mm) thick. Using a 4-inch (10-cm) plain round cutter, cut out 12 rounds. One at a time, transfer them to the prepared muffin pan, easing each one into a cup, pressing down well, and trimming off any overhang. Gather up the scraps, press together, reroll, and, using a small star cutter, cut out 12 stars. Transfer the stars to a parchment-lined plate. Refrigerate the muffin pan and the stars while you make the filling.

To make the filling, in the food processor, combine the butter and sugar and process until creamy. Add the egg, almonds, flour, ginger, mixed spice, and treacle and process until smooth. Place 1 tablespoon of the jam in the base of each tartlet shell and top with 2 generous spoons of the filling. (Alternatively, you can pipe the filling onto the jam.) Place a pastry star in the center of each tartlet.

Bake the tartlets for 5 minutes, then lower the oven temperature to 350°F (180°C) and continue to bake until golden on top, 20–25 minutes. Transfer the pan to a wire rack and brush the top of each tartlet with a little of the ginger syrup to glaze. Let cool for about 10 minutes, then carefully lift each tartlet from the pan. Serve warm.

Chocolate-Dipped Honey and Pecan Anzacs

Anzacs are an Antipodean teatime treat dating back more than a century. They are believed to have originated in Dunedin, New Zealand, and in Australia, they were baked by volunteers and packed in billycans for sending to soldiers during the First World War. Traditionally, they include oats, golden syrup, and coconut. In my interpretation of the recipe, I use locally sourced wildflower honey in place of the golden syrup and substitute muscovado sugar for the refined sugar. The addition of seeds, pecans, and oat bran brings both a light, crunchy crispness and a healthy element to the biscuits.

1 cup (100 g) oats

⅔ cup (80 g) cake flour

⅓ cup (60 g) loosely packed light muscovado sugar

⅓ cup (30 g) oat bran

⅓ cup (30 g) unsweetened shredded dried coconut

½ cup (50 g) pecan halves, roughly chopped

1 tablespoon flaxseed (linseed)

2 tablespoons pumpkin seeds

½ cup plus 1 tablespoon (125 g) butter

3 tablespoons wildflower honey

1 teaspoon pure vanilla extract

½ teaspoon baking soda

1 tablespoon boiling water

4 oz (115 g) dark or milk chocolate, melted and cooled to lukewarm

MAKES ABOUT 30 BISCUITS

Line 2 sheet pans with parchment paper or silicone mats.

In a large bowl, stir together the oats, flour, sugar, oat bran, coconut, pecans, flaxseed, and pumpkin seeds. In a small saucepan over low heat, combine the butter, honey, and vanilla and heat just until the butter melts. Remove from the heat. In a small bowl, dissolve the baking soda in the boiling water, then stir into the butter mixture. Pour the butter mixture into the oat mixture and stir until the dry ingredients are evenly moistened.

Roll teaspoonfuls of the mixture between your palms and place them on the sheet pans, spacing them about 1 inch (2.5 cm) apart. Chill in the refrigerator for 20 minutes. While the dough chills, preheat the oven to 350°F (180°C).

Bake the biscuits until golden, 12–15 minutes. Let cool on the pans on wire racks for 5 minutes, then transfer to the racks and let cool completely.

Dip half of each cooled biscuit into the chocolate and return to a rack. Let stand until set before serving. The biscuits will keep in an airtight container at room temperature for up to 4 days.

Bramble and Apple Jam
with Cinnamon

*A*utumn is a wonderful time for foraging, particularly in the hedgerows, which are home to many varieties of wild fruit, including rowanberries, elderberries, huckleberries, crab apples, and, of course, blackberries, or to use the old country name, brambles. Coming home from a chilly, damp walk with a basket of fat, glistening blackberries is immensely satisfying. This simple, traditional jam is easy to make, and it fills the kitchen with the most wonderful aroma in the process! It is delicious on hot buttered crumpets, which are a vital part of any shoot tea.

1 lb (450 g) blackberries

1 lb (450 g) cooking apples

1 cup (240 ml) water

3⅓ cups (675 g) granulated sugar

Juice of ½ lemon

1 cinnamon stick

1 teaspoon butter

Makes about four ½-pint (240-ml) jars

Wash the canning jars with hot, soapy water, then rinse well in hot water. Place them in a very low oven (210°F/100°C) to dry them completely and to keep them warm until ready to fill. Have ready a couple of saucers for testing the jam.

Sort and rinse the berries, discarding any imperfect ones. Peel, core, and dice the apples. Put the fruit into a large, heavy saucepan, add the water, and bring to a simmer over medium heat. Simmer, stirring often, until the fruit is tender, about 20 minutes.

Add the sugar, lemon juice, and cinnamon, raise the heat to medium-high, and bring to a boil, stirring to dissolve the sugar. Boil for 20 minutes, stirring frequently, then remove from the heat and test if the jam is ready. Drop a spoonful of the jam onto a saucer and put the saucer into the freezer for 5 minutes. Remove from the freezer and gently run your finger through the jam. If it "wrinkles," the jam is ready. If it doesn't, boil for another 5–8 minutes and test again.

Remove and discard the cinnamon stick, then skim off any white "scum" from the top. Add the butter and stir well (this should help to disperse any remaining scum). Carefully ladle the jam into the warmed glass jars. Leave to cool completely before capping and storing.

Children's Afternoon Tea

The façade of Kensington Palace is well recognized around the world. In August 1997, the palace and surrounding gardens were the focus of an extraordinary exhibition of public mourning as thousands upon thousands of people descended on Kensington to lay flowers in memory of Diana, Princess of Wales, who had tragically died in a car crash in Paris. Prior to this, Kensington was not one of the better-known royal palaces in London, though it had been in the royal family since the late seventeenth century.

In the summer of 1689, William III and Queen Mary II needed to find somewhere to live that was away from the smog that regularly enveloped their principal London residence at Whitehall Palace. They purchased Nottingham House, a modest Jacobean mansion, from the Earl of Nottingham. Famed English architect Christopher Wren was retained to draw up plans to enlarge the house. Among his many alterations was a new entrance through an archway surmounted by a clock, which survives to this day. That clock is well known to me, as during my first two years at Kensington Palace as chef to the Duke and Duchess of Gloucester, my bedroom was directly beneath it! At that time, five families were living in the rambling palace, including Princess Margaret, the Queen's sister, and Prince Charles, Princess Diana, Prince William, and Prince Harry.

Some of my fondest memories of my thirteen years in the kitchens at "KP" (as it was fondly known) are of cooking for the two very young princes, William and Harry. Afternoon tea allows more opportunity than any other meal to create tempting and imaginative treats for children. Some of these recipes are inspired by the Queen herself. Jam pennies are an age-old royal tradition and favorite for nursery tea. Although ice cream is not traditionally served for afternoon tea, it is served at Her Majesty's large, annual garden parties at Buckingham Palace (see page 45), which is reason enough to include it in this rather whimsical chapter.

Gingerbread Soldiers in Sentry Boxes

This is my take on a traditional gingerbread house. I was inspired by A. A. Milne's poem about Buckingham Palace and the reference to a sentry box. As the recipe takes some time to make, it is a wonderful project for a rainy afternoon, and with a little help, children can be very creative constructing the sentry box and decorating the soldiers. The gingerbread is delightfully crisp and gingery. It is important not to roll the dough too thickly, as the pieces will be too heavy, and the sentry box will not hold together.

FOR THE GINGERBREAD

½ cup plus 1 tablespoon (125 g) butter, at room temperature

⅔ cup (90 g) loosely packed light brown sugar

⅔ cup (200 g) golden syrup or thick honey

3 cups (375 g) cake flour

1 teaspoon baking soda

2 teaspoons ground ginger

1 teaspoon mixed spice (see Chef's Note)

FOR THE ICING

2 cups plus 2 tablespoons (210 g) sifted confectioners' sugar

1 free-range egg white

½ teaspoon fresh lemon juice

Red, black, and/or blue natural food coloring (optional)

Makes 3 sentry boxes and 12 soldiers

Line 2 large sheet pans with parchment paper or silicone mats.

To make the gingerbread, combine the butter and brown sugar in a food processor and process until pale and creamy. Add the golden syrup, flour, baking soda, ginger, and mixed spice and process until a smooth dough forms.

Turn the dough out onto a lightly floured surface and roll out ⅛ inch (3 mm) thick. Using the template provided on the next page, cut out enough pieces for 3 sentry boxes. Carefully lift the pieces onto a prepared pan. Gather up the scraps, press together, reroll, and cut out 12 soldiers using a cookie cutter. Lift them onto a prepared pan. Place the pans in the refrigerator for 20 minutes to chill the dough. Preheat the oven to 325°F (165°C).

Bake the gingerbread until golden, 8–10 minutes, keeping a careful watch, as the smaller pieces will cook more quickly than the larger ones and will need to be removed from the oven sooner. Let cool on the pans on wire racks for 5 minutes, then transfer the pieces to the racks and let cool completely.

While the gingerbread is baking, make the icing. In a bowl, using an electric mixer, beat together the confectioners' sugar, egg white, and lemon juice on high speed until light and fluffy, 4–5 minutes.

To build the sentry boxes, spoon about one-third of the icing into a piping bag fitted with a plain writing tip no bigger than ⅛ inch (3 mm).

Recipe continues on the following page

Continued from the previous page

 CHEF'S NOTE

Mixed spice is a popular UK ground blend of warm, sweet spices. The formula varies, though it typically includes cinnamon, nutmeg, cloves, allspice, coriander, ginger, and mace. If unavailable, pumpkin pie spice, which is similar, can be substituted.

To assemble the sentry boxes, start by piping a stripe of icing down the left and right edge of each front panel of the sentry boxes. Secure a side panel onto either side of the front panel, using the icing to secure it. Repeat the process for the back panel, piping a stripe of icing down the left and right edge and maneuver it between the side panels, using the icing to secure it. Leave the icing to harden for 10–15 minutes before piping a stripe of icing on the underside of each roof panel along the shorter edges. Attach to the top of the sentry box and leave for 30 minutes to harden. Finish by decorating as desired with more of the icing.

If you wish to decorate the soldiers with icings in different colors, divide the remaining icing into as many small bowls as colors you want to use. Stir enough food coloring into each bowl to achieve the shade you like. For each color, spoon the icing into a piping bag fitted with a ⅛-inch (3-mm) plain or star tip. Alternatively, spoon each icing into a small plastic bag, twist the top closed, and cut off a bottom corner. Decorate the soldiers and sentry boxes as you like, perhaps adding facial features and a jacket, trousers, and a hat to the soldiers and decorative details to the sentry boxes.

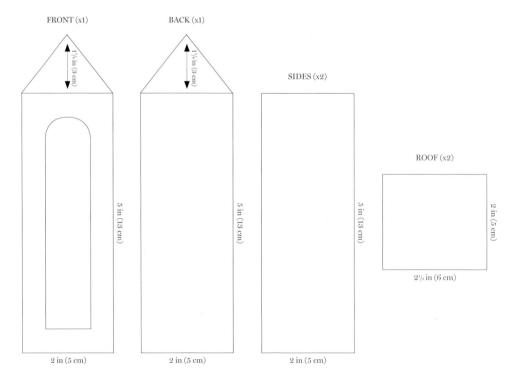

FRONT (x1) 1¼ in (3 cm) 5 in (13 cm) 2 in (5 cm)

BACK (x1) 1¼ in (3 cm) 5 in (13 cm) 2 in (5 cm)

SIDES (x2) 5 in (13 cm) 2 in (5 cm)

ROOF (x2) 2 in (5 cm) 2¼ in (6 cm)

Jam Pennies

*J*am pennies have been enjoyed by generations of royal children for nursery afternoon tea. They can also be made with whole-grain or malted granary bread (see Chef's Note, page 99) and filled with your jam of choice or lemon curd.

6 medium-size slices good-quality fresh white bread

Soft butter

About 12 generous teaspoons raspberry jam

Raspberries, for decorating (optional)

MAKES 12 TEA SANDWICHES

Line up the bread slices on a work surface and butter them. Using a 2-inch (5-cm) plain round cutter, cut out 4 rounds from each bread slice. Spoon 1 generous teaspoon of the jam onto 12 of the bread rounds, spreading it just to the edge. Top with the remaining rounds, butter side down, and press down lightly to secure.

Arrange the sandwiches on a serving plate and decorate the plate with a few raspberries, if desired. Serve at once.

Banana Sandwiches

*I*magine banana slices sprinkled with crunchy demerara sugar nestled between two thick slices of generously buttered, fresh white bread. These are not dainty sandwiches. They are hearty bites for hungry children, as they always disappear off the bread board as soon as they are cut!

1 ripe but firm banana

Soft butter

2 thick slices fresh white bread

Demerara sugar, for sprinkling

MAKES 4 TEA SANDWICHES

Peel the banana, then slice on the diagonal to yield long slices about ½ inch (12 mm) thick. Generously butter the bread slices. Lay the banana slices on a buttered bread slice, covering it completely. Lightly sprinkle the banana slices with the sugar. Top with the second bread slice, butter side down, and press down lightly to secure. Cut the sandwich into quarters on the diagonal and serve right away.

Giant Bourbon Biscuits

*R*ather like giant dominoes, these chocolate sandwich biscuits, filled with a rich, crunchy chocolate filling, are a British classic loved by all ages. They can be made in many shapes and sizes. These are big enough to be a meal in themselves. This recipe, which was my mother's, goes back almost eighty years, so it has been tested on many generations of children, including myself. Commercially made Bourbon biscuits are readily available, but it is worth the effort to make these at home, as they are so much better! Homemade Bourbons were always popular in the royal nursery.

FOR THE BISCUITS

½ cup (115 g) soft butter

1⅓ cups (170 g) cake flour, sifted

1 teaspoon baking powder

3 tablespoons unsweetened cocoa powder

3 tablespoons semolina or polenta

½ cup (100 g) superfine sugar

1 free-range egg

1 teaspoon pure vanilla extract

FOR THE FILLING

4 tablespoons (60 g) butter

⅔ cup (130g) granulated sugar

2 tablespoons unsweetened cocoa powder

½ teaspoon pure vanilla extract

MAKES 12 SANDWICH BISCUITS

To make the biscuits, preheat the oven to 400°F (200°C). Line 2 sheet pans with parchment paper or silicone mats.

In a food processor, combine the butter, flour, baking powder, cocoa powder, and semolina and process until the mixture resembles fine bread crumbs. Add the superfine sugar, egg, and vanilla and process just until the mixture comes together in a smooth dough. Do not overprocess or the biscuits will be very hard.

Turn the dough out onto a lightly floured work surface and roll out the dough into a large rectangle about ¼ inch (6 mm) thick. Using a ruler, cut the dough into rectangles measuring 2 by 3 inches (5 by 7.5 cm). Lift away any scraps and set aside. Using a fork, prick each rectangle to make an attractive pattern of dots. Then, using an offset spatula, carefully transfer the rectangles to the prepared pans, spacing them about 1 inch (2.5 cm) apart. Gather up the scraps, press together, reroll, cut out more rectangles, decorate them with dots, and add them to the pans. You should have 24 rectangles.

Bake the biscuits until firm to the touch, 8–10 minutes. Let cool on the pans on wire racks for 5 minutes, then transfer to the racks and let cool completely.

Recipe continues on the following page

Continued from the previous page

To make the filling, in a small saucepan, melt the butter over low heat. Remove from the heat, add the granulated sugar, cocoa powder, and vanilla, and stir to dissolve the sugar and cocoa powder, mixing well.

When the biscuits are cool, turn 12 of them bottom side up on a work surface. Spread a generous amount of the filling on each overturned biscuit, dividing it evenly and spreading it to the edge. Top with a second biscuit, bottom side down, and press lightly to secure. The biscuits will keep in an airtight container at room temperature for up to 4 days.

👑 CHEF'S NOTE

These biscuits, which are always so popular with children, were first introduced in 1910 under the name Creola. The Bourbon name, dating from the 1930s, comes from the former French royal House of Bourbon.

Mini Chocolate Cups
with Ice Cream and Sprinkles

The only time I have been served ice cream for afternoon tea was at Buckingham Palace, and I can highly recommend it! These tiny chocolate cups, each of which holds just a couple of tablespoons of ice cream, are the perfect addition to a special afternoon tea for little ones. Decorated with colorful sprinkles and miniature Union Jacks, these festive cups are patriotic, playful, and, above all, popular! They can be prepared ahead of time and kept in an airtight container in the freezer, ready to serve when needed.

6 small dark or milk chocolate cups, each about 2 inches (5 cm) in diameter and 1½ inches (4 cm) deep (see Chef's Note)

Vanilla ice cream, for scooping

Brightly colored sugar sprinkles, for topping

6 miniature Union Jacks

Makes 6 filled cups

Put the chocolate cups into the freezer for at least 30 minutes. Fill each chilled cup with a small scoop of ice cream. Top the ice cream with the sugar sprinkles and decorate each cup with a miniature Union Jack. Serve right away or return to the freezer until serving.

 CHEF'S NOTE

If you can't find commercial chocolate cups, they are very easy to make at home: Melt about 3 oz (90 g) dark chocolate or milk chocolate and paint a layer of chocolate onto small silicone molds or onto any small, rigid mold lined with plastic wrap. Chill the molds until the chocolate is set, then paint the molds with a second layer to make the cups sturdier and chill again until set before unmolding. Alternatively, you can paint small foil cupcake liners with chocolate and peel the foil off once the chocolate has hardened.

Hampton Court Palace

All Things Chocolate

Hampton Court, located on the River Thames twelve miles (nineteen kilometers) south of central London, did not begin life as a royal palace. It was built over several years, starting in 1515, by Thomas Wolsey, who was chief minister to Henry VIII and was later appointed a cardinal by Pope Leo X. He was the son of a butcher, and determined to prove his worth, he set about building himself "the finest house in England." It was the largest, boasting over one thousand rooms! Henry VIII and Catherine of Aragon were among the first guests to visit Hampton Court after its completion and were no doubt taken aback by its sheer splendor. A decade later, the palace was gifted to Henry VIII by Cardinal Wolsey, who had fallen from favor, having failed to procure Henry a divorce from Catherine of Aragon.

Almost two hundred years later, in 1690, as part of a rebuilding project at Hampton Court, William III commissioned the building of a kitchen dedicated to chocolate, the first of its kind in Britain. This demonstrated the power and modernity of the monarch, as at that time chocolate was relatively new in the country and was a luxury affordable only to the very wealthy. The king and queen would usually take their chocolate as a drink at breakfast time. It would have been a far cry from the highly processed and frequently overly sweet hot chocolate so common today. The cacao beans would have been roasted, flavored, ground to a paste on a hot stone slab, and then formed into small cakes that were left to mature for several months. They would then have been melted into milk, water, or wine and the drink sweetened with raw sugar and flavored with spices. The Chocolate Kitchen was a secure space where gilded chocolate pots and precious porcelain cups were stored, and it was here that the drink would be poured into serving receptacles before being presented to the king or queen.

This chapter is a celebration of chocolate—the food of kings, not to mention the gods. Raise a toast to William III with a mug of indulgent, specially blended hot chocolate and transport your taste buds back over the centuries with the flavors of the cacao nib nuggets.

The Chocolate Kitchen at Hampton Court.

Chocolate Fudge Cake

This moist, fudgy dark chocolate cake is enveloped in lashings of lightly whipped vanilla and chocolate buttercream and decorated with an abundance of chocolate curls, stars, and sprinkles. It is delicious and easy to make.

FOR THE CAKE

¾ cup (175 g) butter, at room temperature, plus more for the pan

1⅓ cups (175 g) dark brown sugar

1 cup plus 2 tablespoons (150 g) cake flour

5½ tablespoons (30 g) unsweetened cocoa powder

2 teaspoons baking powder

½ teaspoon baking soda

3 free-range eggs, beaten

½ cup (100 g) plain Greek yogurt or sour cream

1 teaspoon pure vanilla extract

FOR THE BUTTERCREAM

6½ tablespoons (90 g) unsalted butter, at room temperature

1½ cups (175 g) confectioners' sugar, sifted

1 teaspoon pure vanilla extract

1 tablespoon whole milk

5½ tablespoons (30 g) unsweetened cocoa powder

FOR THE DECORATION

Selection of chocolate sprinkles, hearts, stars, and curls

Unsweetened cocoa powder, for dusting

SERVES 10

To make the cake, preheat the oven to 325°F (165°C). Butter two 8-inch (20-cm) round cake pans and line the bottom of each pan with parchment paper.

In a bowl, using an electric mixer, beat together the butter and brown sugar on medium speed until light and creamy. Sift together the flour, cocoa powder, baking powder, and baking soda into the bowl, then add the eggs, yogurt, and vanilla and beat on medium speed just until all the ingredients are fully incorporated.

Divide the batter evenly between the prepared pans. Using an offset spatula, smooth the surface of the batter in each pan, then make a shallow hollow in the center so the top is flat when the cake layer emerges from the oven.

Bake the cake layers until the tops spring back to the touch, 25–30 minutes. Let cool in the pans on wire racks for 5 minutes, then invert the pans onto the racks, lift off the pans, turn the layers right side up, and let cool completely.

While the cake layers are baking, make the buttercream. In a medium bowl, using the electric mixer, beat the butter on high speed until light and creamy. Add the confectioners' sugar and vanilla and beat on low speed for a few minutes until combined. Add the milk and continue to beat until incorporated and the buttercream has a light, fluffy consistency. Transfer 6 tablespoons (125 g) of the buttercream to a small bowl. Add the cocoa powder to the buttercream in the medium bowl and beat on medium speed just until incorporated. Cover and set aside both bowls.

To finish the cake, place a layer, top side down, on a serving plate and spread with the vanilla buttercream, extending it to the edge. Top with the second layer, top side up, and spread the chocolate buttercream over the sides and top, smoothing the sides and leaving the top with swirls and peaks. Sprinkle with the chocolate decorations, then dust lightly with the cocoa powder.

The Ultimate Hot Chocolate

This recipe is a nod to William III, who, in the late seventeenth century, was one of the first people in England to enjoy hot chocolate. A luxurious blend of dark chocolate, cocoa powder, spices, and Madagascan vanilla powder, this recipe will change your perspective on hot chocolate forever. It totally eclipses any commercially produced mixes, and yet it takes only a matter of minutes to make. The chocolate marries wonderfully with the cinnamon and nutmeg, the paprika imparts a warming top note, and the enticing yet comforting aroma of vanilla is heavenly. For a very indulgent treat, serve with whipped cream and marshmallows.

FOR THE CHOCOLATE MIX

3½ oz (100 g) dark chocolate

½ cup plus 1 tablespoon (50 g) unsweetened cocoa powder

6½ tablespoons (50 g) confectioners' sugar

1 teaspoon organic pure Madagascan vanilla powder

½ teaspoon ground cinnamon

¼ teaspoon ground nutmeg

Pinch of paprika

TO SERVE

Whole milk, as needed

Whipped cream and marshmallows, for topping (optional)

Makes enough mix
for about 8 servings

To make the mix, using the fine holes on a box grater, grate the chocolate into a small bowl. Add the cocoa powder, sugar, vanilla powder, cinnamon, nutmeg, and paprika and stir to mix well. Transfer to a small jar, cap tightly, and store at room temperature for up to 6 months.

For each serving, heat 1 cup (240 ml) milk in a saucepan over medium heat until almost boiling. Whisk in 2–3 tablespoons of the hot chocolate mix, adjust the heat to maintain a simmer, and simmer, whisking constantly, for 1 minute. Pour into a cup or mug and, if desired, top with some whipped cream and accompany with marshmallows.

Cacao Nib, Date, and Almond Nuggets

I think of these small bites as a raw, healthy version of flapjacks. The lashings of butter, golden syrup, and muscovado sugar found in flapjacks are replaced by coconut oil, a drizzle of maple syrup, and dates, while the cacao nibs deliver intense bursts of flavor and an appealing crunchy texture. Eating a couple of these nuggets is certain to boost your energy, plus they are both vegan and gluten-free. I have included this recipe because the raw earthiness of the cacao is reminiscent of the flavor of the rather primitive hot chocolate served to William III from the Chocolate Kitchen at Hampton Court in the late 1600s.

1 cup (150 g) soft pitted dates, roughly chopped

¾ cup (75 g) ground almonds

½ cup (50 g) gluten-free oats

2½ tablespoons cacao powder (see Chef's Note)

2 tablespoons cacao nibs

3 tablespoons maple syrup

¼ cup (55 g) coconut oil, melted and cooled

1 teaspoon pure vanilla extract

FOR THE DECORATION

¼ cup (30 g) cacao disks, melted and cooled

Makes 20 nuggets

In a food processor, combine the dates, almonds, oats, cacao (not cocoa) powder, and cacao nibs and process until all the ingredients are uniformly ground. Add the maple syrup, coconut oil, and vanilla and pulse a few times to mix well.

Line a sheet pan with parchment paper. Roll tablespoonfuls of the mixture between your palms into tightly compressed nuggets and place on the prepared pan. Chill in the refrigerator for at least 1 hour until firm.

When chilled and firm, dip the top of each nugget into the melted cacao and carefully return the nugget, top side up, to the sheet pan without marring the coating. When all the nuggets are coated, return to the refrigerator for 30 minutes to set the coating. The nuggets will keep in an airtight container in the refrigerator for up to 3 weeks.

 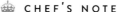 CHEF'S NOTE

In one sense, the two words *cacao* and *cocoa* mean the same thing, as the English word *cocoa* is derived from the Spanish word *cacao*, which is in turn taken from the Nahuatl (Aztecan) word *cacahuatl*. However, there is also a primary difference between the two. Products labeled "cacao", such as cacao powder, are made from beans that have been minimally processed. Cocoa powder is made from cacao beans that have been roasted. Cacao has a stronger and earthier flavor than cocoa, and if substituting cacao powder for cocoa powder in a recipe, reduce the amount by one-third.

Chocolate and Salted Pistachio Cookies

Here is a sophisticated version of the chocolate chip cookie. Rich, crisp on the outside, and moist in the center, they call for dark, slightly bitter chocolate that marries perfectly with the creaminess of the delicately salted pistachios. When served still warm from the oven, they are utterly irresistible. Salted peanuts and peanut butter can be substituted for the pistachios and almond butter.

6 oz (170 g) bittersweet chocolate (70 percent cacao), chopped

5 tablespoons (75 g) butter, at room temperature

3 tablespoons almond butter

1 cup (150 g) loosely packed muscovado sugar

¼ cup (50 g) superfine sugar

1 free-range whole egg plus 1 egg yolk

1 teaspoon pure vanilla extract

1¼ cups (150 g) cake flour

2 tablespoons unsweetened cocoa powder

1 teaspoon baking powder

6½ tablespoons (50 g) salted pistachios, roughly chopped

¼ cup (50 g) white or dark chocolate chunks

½ cup (60 g) confectioners' sugar

MAKES ABOUT 50 COOKIES

Put the chocolate into a small heatproof bowl over (not touching) barely simmering water in a saucepan and heat, stirring occasionally, until the chocolate melts and is smooth. Remove from over the heat and let cool for 5 minutes. Meanwhile, in a large bowl, using an electric mixer, beat together the butter, almond butter, and muscovado and superfine sugars on medium speed until thoroughly combined. Gradually add the whole egg, egg yolk, and vanilla and beat until smooth. Sift together the flour, cocoa powder, and baking powder directly into the bowl. On low speed, beat just until the dry ingredients are thoroughly incorporated. Pour in the cooled chocolate and mix with a wooden spoon or rubber spatula until evenly distributed. Lastly, add the pistachios and chocolate chunks and mix well. Cover the bowl and chill in the refrigerator for 30 minutes.

Preheat the oven to 350°F (180°C). Line 2 sheet pans with parchment paper or silicone mats.

Put the confectioners' sugar into a small bowl. To shape the cookies, roll the dough between your palms into balls the size of a walnut, then toss the balls in the confectioners' sugar until thickly and evenly coated. Arrange the balls on the prepared pans, spacing them about 1 inch (2.5 cm) apart.

Bake the cookies until mostly firm to the touch but still a little soft in the center, about 12 minutes. After 8 minutes, gently press down on each cookie lightly with a fork, to flatten it a little and crack the sugar crust, then continue to bake for about another 4 minutes. Let cool on the pans on wire racks for 5 minutes, then transfer to the racks and let cool completely. The cookies will keep in an airtight container at room temperature for up to 4 days.

Brighton Pavilion

Tea with a Little French Flair

The Royal Pavilion, also known as the Brighton Pavilion, is an exotic palace in the seaside city of Brighton, East Sussex. It is unlike any other British royal palace, combining Regency grandeur with domes and minarets in the style of India and China. It has a colorful history stretching back over two hundred years. Originally built as a seaside pleasure palace for George IV, it has also served as a civic building and as a hospital during the First World War. In 1850, it was sold to the city of Brighton, following Queen Victoria's decision that Osborne House, on the Isle of Wight, should be the royal seaside retreat. Today, the Royal Pavilion is a museum, but its quirky, fanciful appearance means that it will always be a true icon of Brighton.

Two hundred years ago, on January 18, 1817, Prince George hosted a banquet at the Royal Pavilion in honor of Grand Duke Nicolas of Russia. The Prince Regent was famed for his excessive eating and tended to be mocked for his apparent gluttony. The extravagance and the sheer scale of the banquet must surely have impressed the esteemed guest. The menu was designed and executed by the prince's chef, Antonin Carême, one of the "celebrity chefs" of his time, and it included 139 items, some of which sound quite horrifying, such as "Terrine of Larks" and "The Head of a Great

Sturgeon in Champagne." However, in contrast, the "Royal Pavilion rendered in Pastry" was likely quite impressive.

In this chapter, I have re-created four of the less extreme items from that banquet menu for an afternoon tea with a little French flair.

Menu from a royal dinner served at Brighton Pavilion.

Raspberry Swirl Meringues

*T*hese small, rustic meringues have a thin, crunchy shell and a soft, chewy, marshmallow-like center. The addition of freeze-dried raspberry powder to the traditional Parisian recipe imparts a refreshing hit of berry flavor that cuts through the usual sweetness of the meringue. These swirly, gluten-free bites add a lovely splash of color to an afternoon tea spread.

¾ cup (150 g) superfine sugar

2 free-range egg whites

1 teaspoon raspberry vinegar or red wine vinegar

1 tablespoon freeze-dried raspberry powder

2–4 drops red natural food coloring

MAKES ABOUT 30
SMALL MERINGUES

 CHEF'S NOTE

This recipe is based on my favorite meringue formula of weighing the egg whites and then using double the amount of sugar. It is simple and foolproof. I heat the sugar first, as this helps it to dissolve in the egg whites and yield a beautifully glossy, light, stable meringue. The addition of vinegar is what gives these meringues a deliciously chewy center. Before you begin beating the egg whites, make sure the bowl and beater are grease-free or the whites won't thicken.

Preheat the oven to 400°F (200°C). Line a large sheet pan with parchment paper or a silicone mat.

Pour the sugar in a thin, even layer onto the prepared pan. Place the pan in the oven just until the sugar begins to melt around the edges, about 5 minutes, then remove from the oven and set aside.

Lower the temperature to 200°F (100°C) and leave the door slightly ajar to allow the oven to cool down.

While the sugar is heating, beat the egg whites. In a large bowl, using an electric mixer, beat the egg whites on medium speed until stiff peaks form. With the mixer still on medium speed, sprinkle in the warm sugar, a spoonful at a time, beating after each addition until the mixture returns to stiff peaks. Once all the sugar has been incorporated, add the vinegar and beat on high speed for a few minutes. The meringue should be smooth, glossy, and thick.

Sprinkle the raspberry powder onto the meringue, then add 2 drops of the food coloring and stir with a metal spoon to create lovely, vibrant red swirls throughout the meringue, adding another drop or two if needed. Do not mix in the powder and coloring completely. Using 2 teaspoons, place small heaps of the meringue onto the prepared sheet pan, spacing them about 1 inch (2.5 cm) apart.

Bake the meringues until they are dry to the touch and lift easily from the paper or mat, 30–40 minutes. Let cool completely on the pan on a wire rack, then lift off the paper or mat. The meringues will keep in an airtight container at room temperature for up to 2 weeks.

Almond Cake

R icotta, ground almonds, lemon, and polenta give this cake a wonderfully soft texture and zesty flavor. It is the ideal cake for anyone who does not have a sweet tooth. It is also a good choice for those seeking a gluten-free teatime treat.

½ cup plus 2½ tablespoons (150 g) butter, at room temperature, plus more for the pan

1¼ cups (180 g) whole blanched almonds

½ cup (60 g) fine polenta

Finely grated zest of 4 lemons

¾ cup plus 2½ tablespoons (180 g) superfine sugar, plus more for dusting

4 free-range eggs, separated

¾ cup (200 g) whole-milk ricotta cheese

Juice of 2 lemons

Serves 10

Preheat the oven to 300°F (150°C). Butter the sides of a 9-inch (23-cm) round springform pan and line the bottom with parchment paper.

In a food processor, pulse the almonds until finely ground. Add the polenta and lemon zest and process briefly to mix. In a medium bowl, using an electric mixer, beat together the butter and sugar on medium speed until pale and fluffy. Add the egg yolks, one at a time, beating well after each addition. Stir in the almond mixture. In a small bowl, stir together the ricotta and lemon juice, then add to the almond-butter mixture and stir until blended.

In another medium bowl, whisk the egg whites until soft peaks form. Using a rubber spatula, fold the egg whites into the almond-butter mixture just until evenly distributed and no white streaks remain.

Spoon the batter into the prepared pan and smooth the top with an offset spatula. Bake the cake until a toothpick inserted into the center comes out clean, 40–50 minutes. Let cool in the pan on a wire rack for 20 minutes, then unclasp and lift off the sides and, working carefully as the cake is quite delicate, gently transfer the cake, still on the pan bottom. to the rack to cool. Once the cake is completely cool, invert it, lift off the base and parchment, and then turn it upright on a cake plate. Dust the top with sugar before serving.

Apricot, Cherry, and Pistachio Nougat

*T*his classic French confection is not generally served for afternoon tea. But it is certainly not out of place, particularly if you need a gluten-free treat. The cherries and apricots are wonderful little nuggets of tartness nestled in the honey-sweetened nougat, and the pistachios add both color and crunch. Making the nougat recipe requires a little time and patience (and a candy thermometer), but it is well worth the effort. The nougat also makes a lovely edible gift.

2–4 sheets edible rice paper (see Chef's Note)

⅔ cup (100 g) whole blanched almonds

⅔ cup (100 g) peeled pistachios

⅓ cup (50 g) peeled hazelnuts

½ cup (150 g) clear, pourable honey

1½ cups (300 g) superfine sugar

¼ cup (100 g) gluten-free liquid glucose

⅓ cup plus 2 tablespoons (100 ml) water

2 free-range egg whites

1 teaspoon pure vanilla extract

Pinch of salt

¾ cup (100 g) soft dried apricots

⅓ cup (50 g) dried cherries

MAKES 48 PIECES

Preheat the oven to 350°F (180°C). Line the bottom and sides of an 8-inch (20-cm) square pan with rice paper.

Scatter all the nuts in a single layer on a sheet pan. Toast the nuts in the oven, taking care that they don't burn, until they are taking on color, about 10 minutes. Pour onto a plate and set aside.

Put the honey into a small, heavy saucepan. In a second small, heavy saucepan, combine the sugar, glucose, and water. Put the egg whites into a clean bowl, preferably of a stand mixer fitted with the whisk attachment, and whisk on low speed until soft peaks form. At the same time, place the honey over medium heat and heat until it registers 250°F (120°C) on a candy thermometer.

With the mixer still on low speed, pour the hot honey into the egg whites, then increase the speed to medium. While the whites and honey are whisking, place the sugar mixture over medium-high heat and bring to a full boil, then adjust the heat to maintain a steady boil and boil until the syrup registers 293°F (145°C) on the candy thermometer.

Recipe continues on the following page

Continued from the previous page

CHEF'S NOTE

If you prefer nougat that is less sweet, add 2 tablespoons finely grated orange or lemon zest with the nuts and fruit. Liquid glucose, also known as glucose syrup, and edible rice paper can be found in well-stocked grocery stores, specialty shops, and online.

With the mixer still on medium speed, pour the hot sugar syrup in a slow, steady stream into the egg white mixture, then add the vanilla and salt. Continue whisking until you have a thick, glossy, firm meringue (that looks like sticky chewing gum!), about 10 minutes. Don't be tempted to whisk for less than 10 minutes, as you can't whisk the meringue too much but you can whisk it too little.

Stir in all the nuts, the apricots, and the cherries. (If you warm the nuts, it is a little easier to mix them in.) Scrape the mixture into the prepared pan and smooth the surface with an offset spatula. Top the nougat with a sheet of rice paper cut to fit and press down. Leave the nougat to set for at least 2 hours and preferably overnight.

To portion the nougat, turn it out of the pan onto a clean work surface. Have a tall glass of boiling water at hand. Using a long, sharp serrated knife, and dipping the blade into the boiling water before each cut, cut the square into 48 pieces. The nougat will keep in an airtight container at room temperature for up to 1 month.

Banquet in honor of Grand Duke Nicolas of Russia at the Brighton Pavilion.

Salted Caramel Profiteroles

Antonin Carême's menu of January 18, 1817, for the grand banquet at the Royal Pavilion included a tower of profiteroles with aniseed. These traditional choux buns are filled with cream flavored with vanilla (in place of the aniseed) and are enveloped in crisp, glistening caramel. They add a lovely Gallic touch to afternoon tea.

FOR THE CHOUX PASTE

3½ tablespoons (50 g) butter

⅔ cup (150 ml) water

Pinch of fine sea salt

½ cup (60 g) cake flour

1 tablespoon superfine sugar

2 free-range eggs, beaten

FOR THE SAUCE

1 cup (200 g) superfine sugar

2 tablespoons heavy cream, warmed

1 teaspoon pure vanilla extract

Pinch of coarse sea salt

FOR THE FILLING

1 cup (240 ml) heavy cream

2 tablespoons superfine sugar

1 teaspoon pure vanilla extract

MAKES 20 PROFITEROLES

Preheat the oven to 400°F (200°C). Line 2 sheet pans with parchment paper or silicone mats.

To make the choux paste, in a saucepan over medium heat, combine the butter, water, and salt and heat until the butter melts and the mixture comes to a boil. As soon as it boils, remove from the heat and add in the flour all at once. Beat vigorously with a wooden spoon until the mixture is homogenous and smooth, about 2 minutes. Return to medium heat and cook, stirring constantly, until the mixture forms a glossy ball and comes away from the sides of the pan, 2–3 minutes. Remove from the heat and allow to cool a little so the beaten egg, which is added next, doesn't cook.

Add the beaten egg, a little at a time, beating well after each addition until the dough comes back together. When all the egg is incorporated, you should have a smooth paste that drops easily off the lifted spoon. Spoon the choux paste into a large piping bag fitted with a ¾-inch (2-cm) plain tip.

Pipe 20 small balls each about 1 inch (2.5 cm) in diameter onto the prepared pans, spacing them about 1½ inches (4 cm) apart. Smooth the top of each ball with a wet fingertip. Bake the pastries until golden and firm to the touch, 15–20 minutes. Transfer them to a wire rack, turning each one upside down, and let cool completely.

Recipe continues on the following page

Continued from the previous page

While the choux buns are baking and cooling, make the sauce. In a heavy saucepan over medium heat, melt the sugar, swirling the pan gently until the sugar dissolves, turns clear, and starts to bubble. Continue to cook, swirling the pan occasionally to encourage even coloring, until the sugar turns a dark gold, about 5 minutes. Remove from the heat and carefully add the cream and vanilla. The mixture will bubble up. Return the pan to medium heat and whisk constantly with a balloon whisk for about 1 minute to create a smooth, silky sauce. Pour the hot sauce into a small, heatproof bowl and reserve for dipping the choux buns. Keep warm.

To make the filling, in a bowl, using an electric mixer, beat together the cream, sugar, and vanilla on medium speed until stiff peaks form. Spoon the filling into a piping bag fitted with a ¼-inch (6-mm) plain tip.

Using the tip of a sharply pointed knife, make a small hole in the center of the base of each bun. Push the tip of the piping bag through the hole and fill until the choux bun swells.

Carefully dip the top of each filled choux bun into the warm sauce, then return the bun, top side up, to the rack. Let the choux buns sit until the caramel sets before serving. (They can be stacked in a tower for an attractive presentation before the caramel sets.) The filled choux buns are best eaten within a few hours.

Highgrove House

Fresh Herbs from the Garden

Highgrove, in Tetbury, Gloucestershire, is the principal private residence of Prince Charles and the Duchess of Cornwall. HRH purchased the house from the son of former prime minister Harold Macmillan in 1980, the year before he married Diana. It is a classical Georgian house surrounded by incredible gardens, and it made a wonderful family home. When William and Harry were growing up, it was the perfect weekend escape. During the week, they attended school in London and lived at Kensington Palace, where there was only a very small garden. All the space at Highgrove afforded the young princes some much-needed freedom away from the glare of the public eye.

Over the past forty years, Prince Charles has devoted much energy to transforming the estate's gardens. He has worked alongside some talented horticulturalists and designers, personal friends, and the Highgrove team of gardeners. However, he has done much of it himself, and I can bear witness to his passion for his garden. Frequently, at the end of a very long and busy workday, when most people would choose to sit down to their dinner, Prince Charles would don his gardening shoes and go out to work in the garden until it was too dark to continue.

His vision is incredible, evidenced by the presence of not just one garden but a collection of many different landscapes, among them the classic Sundial Garden, the Cottage Garden (which is so quintessentially English yet was inspired by the colors of Tibet), and the wonderfully whimsical Stumpery, which was influenced by Victorian gardening techniques. The walled kitchen garden is perfect, with not a leaf out of place, and somehow also yields the most beautiful organic fruits and vegetables, many of them rare heirloom varieties. The Thyme Walk is a fragrant carpet of twenty or more thyme varieties.

Fresh herbs were central to all the cooking that I did, adding so much character and color to both sweet and savory dishes. I will be forever grateful to Prince Charles for sharing his huge knowledge and passion for herbs with me and by doing so transforming the way that I cooked. I still daydream about my days at Highgrove, when, just minutes before a meal, I would sprint through the wildflower meadow to the walled garden to pick handfuls of fresh herbs! To this day, I can't resist adding a sprig of fresh greenery to almost everything that I make, be it thyme in a lemon cake or mint in a chocolate cake.

Lemon and Thyme Cake

Made with yogurt and olive oil, this cake is incredibly light and yet moist at the same time. While still warm, it is drenched in an aromatic, thyme-infused lemon syrup, which, once cool, forms a delicate, crisp sugary shell on the cake. Served with an abundance of glistening berries, it makes a wonderful centerpiece for a summer afternoon tea in the garden. The aroma of fresh thyme will always bring back indelible memories of the gardens at Highgrove and of the joy of being able to pick fresh herbs just moments before they were put on a cake or in a salad.

FOR THE CAKE

Vegetable oil, for the pan

2⅓ cups (300 g) cake flour, plus more for the pan

¾ cup (180 ml) light olive oil

2 free-range eggs

1 cup (200 g) plain Greek yogurt

1¼ cups (250 g) superfine sugar

2 tablespoons finely grated lemon zest

1 tablespoon baking powder

FOR THE SYRUP

¼ cup (60 ml) fresh lemon juice

6 fresh lemon thyme or common thyme sprigs

⅔ cup (125 g) granulated sugar

FOR THE DECORATION

½ lb (225 g) mixed strawberries, raspberries, blueberries, and/or other seasonal berries

6 fresh lemon thyme or common thyme sprigs

Confectioners' sugar, for dusting

SERVES 10–12

To make the cake, preheat the oven to 350°F (180°C). Oil a 9-inch (23-cm) ring cake pan, carefully covering the entire interior surface, then dust evenly with flour, tapping out the excess.

In a large bowl, whisk together the olive oil, eggs, yogurt, superfine sugar, and lemon zest until well blended. Sift together the flour and baking powder directly into the bowl. Using a large metal spoon or a rubber spatula, stir in the flour mixture just until fully incorporated.

Pour the batter into the prepared pan. Bake the cake until the top is golden and a toothpick inserted near the center comes out clean, 30–35 minutes.

While the cake is baking, make the syrup. In a small saucepan over low heat, warm the lemon juice just until hot. Remove from the heat, add the thyme, and leave to infuse for 20 minutes until cool. Remove and discard the thyme, then stir in the sugar until dissolved.

When the cake is ready, remove from the oven and let cool in the pan on a wire rack for 10 minutes. Then, while the cake is still hot, carefully invert it onto a serving plate. Spoon the syrup over the warm cake, allowing it to run down the sides. Let stand until the syrup sets and the cake has cooled completely.

To decorate, fill the center with the fruits, scatter the thyme on the top, and dust lightly with confectioners' sugar. Serve at once.

White Chocolate and Mint Cake

This eye-catching green-and-white cake with white chocolate–mint buttercream has a wonderful freshness to it. I love the simplicity of the decoration of mint sprigs, which always transports me back to the walled garden at Highgrove. It was a treasure trove of interesting mint varieties, each one with its own particular appearance, aroma, and taste. My favorite varieties include peppermint, spearmint, apple mint, pineapple mint, penny royal mint, Corsican mint, and Egyptian mint, to name but a handful, but the most extraordinary variety of all is chocolate mint, which really does taste of chocolate and is perfect for this cake.

FOR THE CAKE

1½ cups (340 g) butter, at room temperature, plus more for the pans

1¾ cups (350 g) superfine sugar

6 free-range eggs

2¾ cups (340 g) cake flour

4 teaspoons baking powder

Pinch of sea salt

3 tablespoons plain Greek yogurt

1 teaspoon pure vanilla extract

4–6 drops green natural food coloring

FOR THE BUTTERCREAM

1¼ cups (200 g) white chocolate chips

1 cup (225 g) unsalted butter, at room temperature

1¾ cups (225 g) confectioners' sugar, sifted

5 drops pure peppermint oil (see Chef's Note)

Milk, if needed

FOR THE DECORATION

1 small bunch fresh mint, preferably chocolate mint

Confectioners' sugar, for dusting

SERVES 10

To make the cake, preheat the oven to 350°F (180°C). Butter the sides of three 8-inch (20-cm) round cake pans and line the bottom of each pan with parchment paper.

In a large bowl, using an electric mixer, beat together the butter and superfine sugar on high speed until light and creamy. Add 3 of the eggs and beat until fully incorporated. Sift ¼ cup (30 g) of the flour directly into the bowl and beat on medium speed until well mixed. Add the remaining 3 eggs and continue beating until fully incorporated. Sift together the remaining 2½ cups (310 g) flour, the baking powder, and the salt directly into the bowl and, using a metal spoon or a rubber spatula, fold in just until mixed. Lastly, mix in the yogurt and vanilla.

Spoon one-third of the batter into a prepared pan. Stir 2 drops, or more if required, of the food coloring into the remaining batter to create a pale green. Spoon half of the pale green batter into a second prepared pan. Add a few more drops food coloring to the remaining batter to create a deeper green and then spoon the deep green batter into the third prepared pan. Using an offset spatula, smooth the surface of the batter in each pan, then make a small hollow in the center so the top is flat when the cake layer emerges from the oven.

Recipe continues on the following page

Continued from the previous page

 CHEF'S NOTE

I use food-grade peppermint oil rather than peppermint extract to flavor the icing. It has a very intense flavor and only a few drops are needed. It gives the icing a much fresher and more authentic flavor than peppermint extract, which contains alcohol.

Bake the cake layers until the tops spring back to the touch and a toothpick inserted into the center of each cake comes out clean, 20–25 minutes.

While the cake layers are baking, make the buttercream. Put the chocolate chips into a small heatproof bowl over (not touching) barely simmering water in a saucepan and heat, stirring occasionally, until the chocolate melts and is smooth. Remove from over the heat and let cool completely.

In a bowl, using the electric mixer, beat the butter on low speed until creamy. Gradually add the confectioners' sugar while continuing to beat on low speed until fully combined, then beat in the peppermint oil. Pour in the cooled chocolate and continue to beat on low speed until the buttercream has a soft, spreadable consistency. (Be sure the chocolate is completely cool before adding it, or the buttercream will melt.) If the buttercream is too thick, add a few drops of milk to make it softer. Cover and reserve until needed.

When the cake layers are ready, let cool in the pans on wire racks for 5 minutes, then invert the pans onto the racks, lift off the pans, turn the layers right side up, and let cool completely.

To assemble the cake, trim the tops of the cake layers so they will sit flat, if necessary. Place the white layer, top side down, on a serving plate. Spread with a generous layer of buttercream, extending it to the edge. Top with the pale green layer, spread with a generous layer of buttercream, and then top with the deep green layer. Spread a generous layer of buttercream on the top of the cake and a thin layer of buttercream around the sides, finishing the top and sides smoothly and neatly.

To decorate, place the mint bunch in the center on the top of the cake, then dust the top lightly with confectioners' sugar. The mint may wilt if the weather is warm; to prevent this, put it in water in a tiny glass container before setting it on the cake. If you have mint growing in the garden, you can also clip the pretty flowers on the plants and use them to decorate along with the leaves. Serve at once.

Goat Cheese, Zucchini, and Chive Muffins

*T*hese wonderfully savory, little muffins are a welcome departure from tea sandwiches. You can ring the changes with the cheese, using your favorite goat cheese, Swiss Gruyère, or even a feisty British blue like Stilton. Serve with farmhouse butter, cream cheese, or homemade pesto (see palmiers recipe on page 81).

Butter, at room temperature, for the pans

2 ⅓ cups (300 g) cake flour

4 teaspoons baking powder

½ teaspoon sea salt

¼ teaspoon paprika

½ cup (50 g) grated sharp (mature) Cheddar cheese

3 tablespoons freshly grated Parmesan cheese

2 tablespoons pine nuts

¾ cup plus 2 tablespoons (200 ml) whole milk

2 free-range eggs

1 tablespoon canola oil or melted butter

¾ cup (150 g) grated zucchini

4 oz (115 g) soft-ripened goat cheese from a log, cut into ¼-inch (6-mm) cubes

3 tablespoons finely chopped fresh chives

Makes 36 muffins

Preheat the oven to 400°F (200°C). Butter three 12-cup mini muffin pans. Cut 36 strips of parchment paper each ½ inch (12 mm) wide and 4 inches (10 cm) long. Place a strip in each of the muffin cups, extending the ends over the rim. The parchment makes it easier to remove the muffins from the pans once they are baked.

Sift together the flour, baking powder, salt, and paprika into a bowl. Add the Cheddar and Parmesan cheeses and the pine nuts and stir to mix. Make a well in the center of the flour mixture. In a large measuring pitcher, whisk together the milk, eggs, oil, and zucchini just until blended. Pour the milk mixture into the well in the flour mixture. Set aside 36 cubes of the goat cheese for topping the muffins. Add the remaining goat cheese cubes and the chives to the well and gently stir together the wet and dry ingredients just until evenly blended. Do not overmix.

Spoon the batter into the prepared pans, dividing it evenly among the cups. Place a goat cheese cube on top of each muffin. Bake for 5 minutes, then turn down the oven temperature to 375°F (190°C) and continue to bake for 10–12 minutes longer. The muffins should be well risen, golden, and spring back to the touch. Let cool in the pans on wire racks for a few minutes, then lift out the muffins and let cool on the racks. Serve warm. The muffins will keep in an airtight container at room temperature for up to 2 days.

Garden Herb Pesto Palmiers

*S*o light, so crisp, and so summery, these savory pastries are even more moreish than sweet palmiers. They are very easy to make, and you will find they will start to disappear the minute they exit the oven! I use homemade pesto, as the flavor and color are worlds better than those of a commercially made one, especially if you can use homegrown herbs.

FOR THE PESTO

¼ cup (30 g) pine nuts

¾ cup (90 g) freshly grated Parmesan cheese

1 small clove garlic

2½ cups (75 g) loosely packed fresh basil leaves

3 tablespoons olive oil

Freshly ground black pepper

1 sheet all-butter puff pastry, about 11½ oz (320 g), thawed according to package directions if frozen

Flour, for dusting

¼ cup (30g) freshly grated Parmesan cheese

MAKES ABOUT 30 PALMIERS

Preheat the oven to 375°F (190°C). Line 2 sheet pans with parchment paper or silicone mats.

To make the pesto, in a food processor, combine the pine nuts, Parmesan, and garlic and pulse until finely chopped. Add the basil, oil, and a few twists of pepper and process until a spreadable mixture forms. Spoon the pesto into a jar (see Chef's Note).

Lay the pastry sheet on a lightly floured work surface and roll out into a rectangle measuring about 10 by 16 inches (25 by 40 cm). Spread enough of the pesto onto the pastry to create a thin, even layer, extending it to the edges. Sprinkle with most of the Parmesan. Fold one of the long sides over to the center of the sheet and then fold the opposite side over to meet in the center. Spread more pesto on the folded pastry, again extending it to the edges, and sprinkle with the remaining Parmesan. Fold the long sides over to meet in the center again and then fold the pastry strip in half so it is 8 inches (20 cm) long. Chill in the refrigerator for 20 minutes.

Using a sharp, thin knife, carefully slice the filled pastry crosswise into slices about 1/4 inch (6 mm) wide. Lay the slices flat on the prepared pans, spacing them about 1 inch (2.5 cm) apart. Bake the palmiers, turning them over after about 10 minutes to crisp the second side, until golden, about 15 minutes. Let cool for a few minutes on the pans on wire racks. They are best when eaten while still warm from the oven.

 CHEF'S NOTE

You can use a combination of fresh herbs and tender greens in the pesto. For example, basil, chives, mint, and arugula go together well. You will have more pesto than you need. Refrigerate the leftover, tightly capped, for up to 1 week and use for pasta or in salads or sandwiches.

Blenheim Palace

Winston Churchill's Teatime Favorites

Located in Woodstock, in Oxfordshire, Blenheim Palace, an exceptionally large country house, is the seat of the Dukes of Marlborough, with the twelfth Duke of Marlborough currently in residence. Built between 1705 and 1722, and surrounded by two thousand acres (eight hundred hectares) of landscaped parkland and formal gardens, it is the only country house in England to hold the title of palace that is home to neither royalty nor a bishop. Sir Winston Churchill, the grandson of the seventh Duke of Marlborough, was born at Blenheim Palace in 1874 and spent a considerable amount of time there throughout his life.

The recipes in this chapter are all inspired by Churchill's incredible cook, Georgina Landemare, who began working in kitchens at just fifteen years old and didn't stop until she was seventy-three. She wrote to the Churchills in 1939 and offered herself as their wartime cook. She then worked for the family from 1940 to 1954, a period in which rationing was in force in Britain. Her ability to create extravagant meals from limited supplies and to adapt to Churchill's hectic schedule made her a highly valued member of the household. Churchill loved his food, not only for pleasure but also as a diplomatic tool in a time when the world was in the depths of war. It was most important that he was not seen to be getting special treatment during rationing, which is why Mrs.

Landemare's extraordinary resourcefulness in the kitchen was so highly respected.

Although these recipes are drawn from the war and postwar period, they are not as simple or economical as they would have been during those years of extreme shortages. They are all, however, a nod to an incredible leader and the power behind him, his fantastic cook! And they can all be made by hand, just as they would have been in Mrs. Landemare's day.

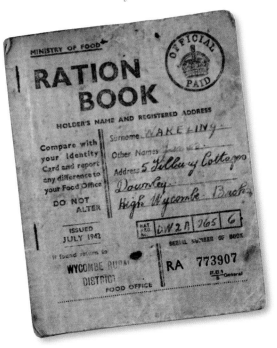

A typical government-issued wartime food ration book.

Glazed Ginger Shortbread

*T*his *"melt and mix" shortbread is quick to make. The stem ginger makes it moister than traditional shortbread, and the spelt flour adds a delightful nuttiness. The combination of the ground ginger and stem ginger gives it a lovely, hearty warmth. This shortbread can also be baked in a 9-inch (23-cm) round pan and sliced into wedges.*

FOR THE SHORTBREAD

½ cup plus 2½ tablespoons (150 g) butter

½ cup (100 g) demerara sugar

2 teaspoons ground ginger

1 cup (125 g) cake flour

½ cup (60 g) spelt flour

1 teaspoon baking powder

2 bulbs (40 g) stem ginger in syrup, finely grated

FOR THE GLAZE

4 tablespoons (60 g) butter

1 tablespoon syrup from stem ginger

½ teaspoon ground ginger

½ cup (60 g) confectioners' sugar, sifted

1 bulb stem ginger in syrup, finely grated

MAKES 24 PIECES

To make the shortbread, preheat the oven to 350°F (180°C). Line an 8-inch (20-cm) square cake pan with parchment paper.

In a saucepan large enough to hold all the ingredients, melt the butter over low heat. Remove from the heat and, using a wooden spoon, stir in the demerara sugar and the ground ginger, then continue stirring until the mixture thickens and becomes like a glossy butterscotch sauce. Sift together both flours and the baking powder directly into the saucepan and stir just until well mixed. Lastly, add the stem ginger and stir until combined.

Scrape the mixture out into the prepared pan and smooth the top with the back of the spoon. Bake the shortbread until the top is lightly golden, 15–20 minutes.

While the shortbread is baking, make the glaze. In a small saucepan over low heat, melt the butter with the ginger syrup and ground ginger. Remove from the heat and beat in the confectioners' sugar and grated ginger.

When the shortbread is ready, transfer the pan to a wire rack. Pour the glaze over the warm shortbread. Then, using an offset spatula, evenly spread the glaze to the edges of the pan, smoothing the surface. Cut the shortbread into 24 pieces. Let cool completely before removing from the pan. The shortbread will keep in an airtight container at room temperature for up to 4 days.

 CHEF'S NOTE

If stem ginger in syrup is unavailable, use crystallized ginger and substitute honey for the syrup. The shortbread will be crispier and crunchier and equally delicious.

Caramel Apple Turnovers

*T*raditionally, turnovers are shaped by folding a piece of dough over a filling and sealing the edges closed. Originally made as a "portable meal," they can be sweet or savory and shaped as triangles, half-moons, or squares. During the wartime years, these fruit-filled pastries would have been made in autumn when people picked apples off a tree in their garden, as fruit was strictly rationed. The salted caramel is my addition to this classic recipe. Serve these simple turnovers of cinnamon-scented apples enveloped in crisp layers of buttery puff pastry warm from the oven.

FOR THE FILLING

2 tablespoons butter

1 tablespoon light muscovado sugar

3 Braeburn apples, peeled, cored, and diced

½ teaspoon ground cinnamon

FOR THE CARAMEL

⅓ cup (75 g) superfine sugar

2 tablespoons water

½ cup plus 1 tablespoon (125 g) crème fraîche

3 tablespoons light muscovado sugar

1 teaspoon pure vanilla extract

Pinch of salt

1 sheet all-butter puff pastry, about 11½ oz (320 g), thawed if frozen

Flour, for dusting

1 free-range egg, beaten, for the glaze

Confectioners' sugar, for dusting

MAKES 8 TURNOVERS

Preheat the oven to 400°F (200°C). Line a large sheet pan with parchment paper or a silicone mat.

To make the filling, in a heavy saucepan over medium heat, melt the butter with the muscovado sugar. Add the apples and cinnamon and cook, stirring often, for a few minutes, until the apples soften. Remove from the heat and let cool.

To make the caramel, in a small, heavy saucepan over low heat, combine the superfine sugar and water and heat gently, stirring to dissolve the sugar. When the sugar has dissolved, stop stirring, bring to a boil, and boil, swirling the pan occasionally to encourage even coloring, until the sugar turns a rich amber, about 4 minutes. Remove from the heat and carefully add the crème fraîche, muscovado sugar, vanilla, and salt. The mixture will bubble up. Return the pan to low heat and stir with a wooden spoon for another minute, then pour into a small, heatproof bowl and let cool.

Recipe continues on the following page

Continued from the previous page

To make the turnovers, lay the pastry sheet on a lightly floured work surface and roll out into a 16-inch (40-cm) square no more than ¼ inch (6 mm) thick. Cut out sixteen 4-inch (10-cm) squares. Place a spoon of the filling onto the center of 8 squares, leaving a ¾-inch (2-cm) border around the edge and using up all the filling. Brush the border of each square with water. Gently fold each of the remaining 8 squares in half on the diagonal to form a triangle. Using a sharp, floured knife, make 4 small diagonal cuts along the folded pastry edge, then gently unfold each triangle, returning it to a square.

Place the decorated squares over the bases and press down along the edges to seal. Brush the tops with the beaten egg, being careful not to let it run down the sides, as it will prevent the pastry from rising. Bake the turnovers until well risen, crisp, and golden, 20–25 minutes. Let cool on the pan on a wire rack for a few minutes, then dust lightly with confectioners' sugar and serve warm.

Seville Orange Marmalade Cake

*W*e *are led to believe that traditional Seville orange marmalade was a staple in Winston Churchill's diet, no doubt eaten on hot buttered toast for breakfast. This cake is always enjoyed by marmalade lovers. Made with whole-grain spelt flour and with maple syrup in place of sugar, it is light but slightly nutty in texture and is not too sweet. It is finished with a delicious orange-infused, crunchy topping.*

FOR THE CAKE

¾ cup plus 1½ tablespoons (190 g) butter, at room temperature, plus more for the pan

1 ½ cups (190 g) spelt flour

2 teaspoons baking powder

2 free-range eggs

3 tablespoons Seville orange marmalade

1 tablespoon finely grated orange zest

¾ cup (325 g) maple syrup

FOR THE TOPPING

1 tablespoon butter, melted

¼ cup superfine sugar

2 tablespoons finely grated orange zest

1 teaspoon pure vanilla extract

Pinch of salt

SERVES 10

To make the cake, preheat the oven to 350°F (180°C). Butter an 8 x 4 x 2½-inch (20 x 10 x 6-cm) loaf pan and line the bottom with parchment paper.

In a bowl, using a wooden spoon or an electric mixer, beat the butter until very soft and creamy. Add the flour, baking powder, eggs, marmalade, orange zest, and maple syrup and beat until all the ingredients until well mixed.

Spoon the batter into the prepared pan and smooth the top with an offset spatula. Bake the cake until the top is golden and a toothpick inserted into the center comes out clean, 45–50 minutes. Let cool in the pan on a wire rack for a few minutes, then invert the pan onto the rack, lift off the pan, and turn the cake upright.

To make the topping, in a small bowl, stir together the butter, sugar, orange zest, vanilla, and salt until the sugar dissolves. Using the offset spatula, spread it evenly over the top of the warm cake. Serve the cake once it has cooled.

Churchill's Fruit Cake

According to Georgina Landemare, Churchill's cook, fruit cake was a great favorite of the prime minister's. This recipe is inspired by one that appears in Mrs. Landemare's Churchill's Cookbook. *It is lighter and more colorful, and glacé cherries, dried figs, and dried apricots replace the golden raisins (sultanas). Some eighty years ago, the fruit was soaked in tea to soften it. However, I use apple juice and also add in a whole grated apple, which help to make this cake pleasantly moist.*

1 cup (240 ml) apple juice

1½ cups (200 g) soft dried apricots, diced

1 cup (225 g) butter, at room temperature

¾ cup (170 g) firmly packed dark brown sugar

2 tablespoons black treacle or honey

5 free-range eggs

2¼ cups (285 g) cake flour

1 tablespoon baking powder

2 teaspoons mixed spice (see Chef's Note, page 38)

1 medium apple, unpeeled, grated on the large holes of a box grater

¾ cup (110 g) glacé cherries, halved and dusted in flour

½ cup (70 g) soft dried figs, diced

2 tablespoons granulated sugar

SERVES 12

 CHEF'S NOTE

As long as you have room-temperature butter, it is very easy to make this cake by hand, as Georgina Landemare no doubt did.

Preheat the oven to 300°F (150°C). Line an 8-inch (20-cm) square springform or loose bottom pan with 3-inch (7.5-cm) sides with parchment paper.

In a small saucepan over high heat, bring the apple juice to a boil. Remove from the heat, add the apricots, and leave to soak for at least a few hours or preferably overnight to plump the fruit.

In a bowl, using a wooden spoon, cream together the butter and brown sugar until light and fluffy. Add the treacle and beat to mix well. Then add the eggs, one at a time, mixing well after each addition. If the mixture begins to curdle, add a couple of spoons of the flour.

Sift together the (remaining) flour, baking powder, and mixed spice directly into the butter mixture, then stir just until all the flour mixture is evenly incorporated. Drain the apricots, reserving the apple juice, and add the apricots, grated apple, cherries, and figs to the batter and mix to distribute evenly.

Spoon the batter into the prepared pan. Using an offset spatula, smooth the surface, then make a small hollow in the center so the top is flat when the cake emerges from the oven.

Bake the cake until a toothpick inserted into the center comes out clean, 1¼–1½ hours. If the top is becoming too dark before the cake is done, cover it loosely with aluminum foil or parchment paper. Let cool in the pan on a wire rack for 5 minutes, then remove the pan sides.

While the cake is cooling, pour the reserved apple juice into a small saucepan, add the granulated sugar, and place over medium heat. Bring to a simmer, stirring to dissolve the sugar, and simmer for a few minutes until syrupy. Remove from the heat and paint the syrup over the top and sides of the warm cake. Let cool completely before serving.

Balmoral Castle

Scottish Salmon

Balmoral Castle, located in Royal Deeside, Scotland, lies alongside the meandering River Dee and almost in the shadow of Lochnagar Mountain. It is the main residence of the 50,000-acre (22,200-hectare) royal estate that is privately owned by the Queen (it does not form part of the Crown Estate) and is greatly loved by everyone in the family, as it provides a much-needed escape from the very public lives that they all lead. Every summer, the Queen, along with many other family members, visits Balmoral for an extended break. They immerse themselves in the "Highland life" of walking, fishing, stalking, painting, foraging, and enjoying local events like the famous Braemar games.

Prince Albert bought the original castle and estate in 1852. Queen Victoria was reportedly inspired to spend more time in Scotland after reading Lord Byron's words, which so accurately describe this beautiful and rugged corner of the Scottish Highlands:

> England, thy beauties are tame and domestic
> To one who has roamed over mountains afar
> Oh! For the crags that are wild and majestic
> The steep frowning glories of dark Lochnagar.

In 1853, work began on building a new, bigger castle. Constructed of gray granite from a nearby quarry, it was designed in the Scottish baronial style. On its completion in 1856, the original castle was demolished. Over the years, successive members of the royal family have purchased more land to increase the size of this working estate, which today includes forestland, farmland, grouse moors, and managed herds of deer, ponies, and the fabulous woolly Highland cattle.

Balmoral was a magical place to work as a chef. We always stayed close by at Birkhall House, which belonged to the Queen Mother and now belongs to Prince Charles. There is an abundance of amazing wild produce to be foraged on the estate, including chanterelles, cèpes, garlic, wood sorrel, blackberries, and elderflowers. I spent many a happy hour in the woods seeking out wild mushrooms, of which there are numerous varieties in Scotland. The beautiful River Dee, where fly fishing is a popular pastime, is one of the finest salmon waterways in Europe. Here are four of my favorite recipes for using salmon, all of which will bring a taste of the Scottish Highlands to afternoon tea.

Potted Salmon

This is a great way to use up small trimmings of salmon. Combined with plenty of fresh herbs, lemon zest, and coarse black pepper, and served with rustic malted granary toast, it makes a hearty afternoon tea treat fit for a king!

8½ oz (240 g) skinless salmon fillet, pin bones removed

Sea salt and freshly coarse-ground black pepper

1 lemon, thinly sliced, plus finely grated zest and juice of 1 lemon

1 fresh thyme sprig

2 fresh dill sprigs, 1 left whole and 1 finely chopped

1 tablespoon olive oil

6 tablespoons (85 g) butter

1 tablespoon finely chopped fresh chives

4 tiny fresh flat-leaf parsley sprigs

Malted granary bread toast, cut into triangles, for serving (see Chef's Note)

SERVES 4

Preheat the oven to 350°F (180°C).

Place the salmon in a small baking dish. Season with a pinch of salt and a few twists of pepper. Lay the lemon slices over the salmon, then top with the thyme sprig and the whole dill sprig. Drizzle the oil over the fish. Cover the dish with aluminum foil, place in the oven, and bake the fish until cooked through, about 15 minutes. Remove from the oven and let the fish cool completely, leaving the dish covered.

To clarify the butter, in a small saucepan, melt the butter over medium heat, then allow it to bubble as you skim off all the white froth that forms on the surface. Pour into a small, heatproof clear container and allow the sediment to sink to the bottom.

When the salmon is cool, flake it into a bowl, checking for and discarding any errant bones. Taste and adjust the seasoning with salt and pepper if needed. Add the lemon zest, 2 teaspoons of the lemon juice, the chives, and the chopped dill and mix well. Divide the salmon mixture evenly among 4 small ramekins, then press down with the back of a spoon so the surface is smooth. Carefully spoon the cooled clarified butter onto the salmon, dividing it evenly and leaving the sediment behind. Top each ramekin with a sprig of parsley. Chill in the refrigerator for at least 2 hours to set the butter, then serve with the toast.

 CHEF'S NOTE

Malted granary bread is a traditional English loaf made from white and whole-wheat flours and cracked malted barley and wheat. Any dark, flavorful, hearty bread, such as sprouted grain bread, can be substituted.

Mini Oatcakes with Gravlax and Crème Fraîche

*O*atcakes can almost be considered a staple of the Scottish diet. These traditional, earthy biscuits lend themselves to being served at any time of the day, depending on what they are topped with. The rough texture of this version is complemented perfectly by the rich, velvety gravlax and crème fraîche. But these rustic miniature oatcakes are just as good with farmhouse butter, cheese, jam, or honeycomb. Oatcakes are traditionally round, but they can be made in any shape, from scalloped rounds to squares, hearts, or even stars!

FOR THE OATCAKES

1½ cups (150 g) rolled oats

⅓ cup (50 g) oat bran

½ teaspoon baking soda

½ teaspoon sea salt

Freshly ground black pepper (optional)

2 tablespoons butter, melted

2 teaspoons runny honey

About 6 tablespoons (90 ml) hot water

Flour, for dusting

FOR THE TOPPING

¼ cup (60 g) crème fraîche

4 oz (115 g) gravlax

36 tiny fresh dill sprigs

MAKES 36 TOPPED OATCAKES

 CHEF'S NOTE

You can make the dough in a food processor rather than by hand, but the texture of the oats will be lost; if the dough is overprocessed, the oatcakes will be hard.

To make the oatcakes, preheat the oven to 350°F (180°C). Line 2 sheet pans with parchment paper or silicone mats.

Using a food processor, process 1 cup (100 g) of the oats until they are the texture of fine bread crumbs. Pour them into a large bowl, add the remaining ½ cup (50 g) oats, the oat bran, baking soda, salt, and a few twists of pepper, and stir to mix. Make a well in the center of the oat mixture and add the butter, honey, and 4 tablespoons (60 ml) of the water to the well. Using a wooden spoon, draw the oat mixture into the liquid ingredients and mix until a rough dough forms. If the mixture is too dry to shape, add more water as needed to create a dough that you can form into a ball but is not sticky. Use your hands to bring the dough together.

On a lightly floured work surface, roll out the dough ⅛ inch (3 mm) thick. Using a 2-inch (5-cm) cutter of any shape, cut out as many oatcakes as possible and transfer them to the prepared pans, spacing them about 1 inch (2.5 cm) apart. Gather up the scraps, press together, reroll, cut out more cakes, and add them to the pans. When you press together the scraps, you may need to add a little bit of water, as the dough dries out quickly. You should have 36 oatcakes.

Bake the oatcakes until golden, 10–15 minutes. Let cool on the pans on wire racks for 5 minutes, then transfer to the racks and let cool completely.

To serve, top each oatcake with a small dollop of crème fraîche, a twist of gravlax, and a sprig of dill.

Smoked Salmon, Asparagus, and Cream Cheese Wraps

A *welcome change from traditional smoked salmon tea sandwiches, these little wraps can be made in advance and sliced just before serving.*

4 corn tortillas, each about 7 inches (18 cm) in diameter

4 tablespoons (60 g) cream cheese

7 oz (200 g) smoked salmon, thinly sliced

½ lemon

Freshly ground black pepper

12 long asparagus spears, trimmed and lightly cooked

Handful of baby salad leaves

Fresh dill sprigs and dill flowers (if available), for garnish

MAKES 24 PIECES

Lay the corn tortillas on a work surface. Spread the cream cheese on the tortillas, extending the edges. Lay the salmon on top in an even layer. Squeeze a little lemon juice over the salmon, then sprinkle with pepper. Lay 3 asparagus spears lengthwise down the center of each tortilla and top with a few salad leaves. Starting from the edge nearest you, roll up each tortilla tightly, then trim off about ½ inch (12 mm) from each end and discard. Wrap each roll in parchment paper or plastic wrap and chill in the refrigerator for at least 30 minutes or for up to 4 hours.

To serve, slice each wrap crosswise into six 1-inch (2.5-cm) pieces. Arrange on a plate and garnish with dill sprigs and dill flowers (if available).

Tartlets of Hot-Smoked Salmon with Green Onions and Ruby Chard

*T*ender flakes of hot-smoked salmon nestled into a rich egg custard and encased in fine crisp layers of filo pastry—these tartlets are heavenly. Served straight from the oven, they always disappear quickly, especially on cold winter afternoons.

6 large sheets filo pastry, thawed according to package directions if frozen

Flour, for dusting

4 tablespoons (60 g) butter, melted

FOR THE FILLING

9 oz (250 g) hot-smoked salmon fillet

¾ cup (180 ml) heavy cream or half-and-half (single cream)

2 free-range egg yolks

1 tablespoon finely chopped fresh chives

Sea salt and freshly ground black pepper

4 green onions, white and green parts, very thinly sliced

Handful of baby red chard leaves

Cayenne pepper, for dusting

Makes 12 tartlets

Preheat the oven to 350°F (180°C). Place twelve 2-inch (5-cm) round tartlet molds on a sheet pan.

Lay a filo sheet on a lightly floured work surface, keeping the other sheets covered with plastic wrap to prevent them from drying out. Lightly brush the entire sheet with some of the butter. Lay a second sheet on top and cut the layered sheets into 4 equal squares. Repeat with the remaining 4 filo sheets to make 12 squares total. Line each tartlet mold with a filo square, pressing the filo down firmly onto the base. Chill in the refrigerator while you ready the filling ingredients.

Flake the salmon into a small bowl, removing and discarding any errant bones. In a second small bowl, whisk together the cream and egg yolks until blended, then whisk in the chives and season with salt and black pepper. Sprinkle an equal amount of the green onions onto the bottom of each tartlet shell. Cover with the salmon and then the chard leaves, dividing them both evenly. Divide the egg mixture evenly among the tartlet shells, pouring it over the salmon and chard. Dust the tops lightly with the cayenne.

Bake the tartlets until well puffed and golden, 12–15 minutes. Serve at once.

 CHEF'S NOTE

A 12-cup mini muffin pan can be used in place of the tartlet molds.

Crofter's Fare

This wonderfully remote castle is located in Caithness, on the north coast of Scotland, about six miles (ten kilometers) west of the village of John o'Groats. When the weather is clear, the Orkney Islands are visible to the north. Formerly known as Barrogill Castle, it was built in the sixteenth century. It was in poor repair when it was purchased by HM Queen Elizabeth The Queen Mother in 1952, shortly after the death of her husband, George VI. She acquired it for use as a holiday retreat and soon ordered its restoration, a costly project that took some two years and included outfitting it with electricity and running water for the first time. The Castle of Mey Trust is now under the stewardship of Prince Charles, who continues to restore, develop, and preserve the castle and the surrounding estate. It is a place much loved by Prince Charles, partly due to its connection with his beloved grandmother but also because of its beautiful and isolated location.

This chapter is devoted to simple traditional Scottish fare of the type that would have been enjoyed by local crofters in the area surrounding the castle. Crofting is a form of land tenure and small-scale food production that is particular to the Scottish Highlands and the islands of Scotland, such as Shetland and the Orkneys. The life of a crofter in centuries past was a hard one due to the harsh local climate and to the challenging nature of the landscape for agriculture. All of these Scottish specialties would be greatly enjoyed with a big mug of tea at the end of a long day of working in the fields.

A classic view of the Scottish Highlands.

Scotch Pancakes

These traditional Scottish pancakes are also known as drop scones, as the batter is "dropped" onto a hot pan to cook. They are a popular teatime treat in Scotland and are also enjoyed by the royal family. Some sixty years ago, when US President Dwight Eisenhower was the guest of Queen Elizabeth in Scotland, he was served Scotch pancakes made according to her family recipe. He subsequently received a typed copy of the recipe, which is now preserved in the National Archives of the United States.

1¾ cups (225 g) cake flour

¼ cup (50 g) superfine sugar

2 teaspoons baking powder

Pinch of salt

2 free-range eggs, plus whole milk to total 1¼ cups (300 ml)

1 teaspoon pure vanilla extract

Vegetable oil, for the frying pan

Butter and jam of choice or honey, for serving

MAKES 24 SMALL PANCAKES

Sift together the flour, sugar, baking powder, and salt into a bowl. Crack the eggs into a measuring pitcher, whisk briefly to blend, and then add the milk as needed to total 1¼ cups (300 ml) and the vanilla. Make a well in the flour mixture and pour the egg mixture into it. Using a balloon whisk, mix the dry ingredients into the liquid ingredients, gradually drawing them in from the edge of the bowl. Continue mixing until you have a smooth, lump-free batter. Leave to stand at room temperature for 30 minutes.

Heat a nonstick frying pan over medium heat and add 1½ teaspoons oil. When the oil is hot, add a tablespoon of batter to the hot pan for each pancake, being careful not to crowd them. Cook until bubbles begin to appear on the surface, about 1 minute, then flip the pancakes and cook until golden on both sides, about 1 minute longer. Transfer to a plate and keep warm. Cook the remaining batter the same way, adding more oil to the pan as needed.

Serve the pancakes warm with butter and jam or honey on the side.

Butteries

A rustic, unsophisticated Scottish version of a French croissant, butteries are a specialty of the northeastern corner of Scotland, where they are found in every baker's shop. These savory rolls are most commonly eaten warm for breakfast with butter and marmalade. However, this "cocktail-size" version makes a wonderful addition to a hearty country tea.

3⅔ cups (450 g) bread flour

1 heaping teaspoon salt

3 tablespoons active dry yeast

1 teaspoon granulated sugar

1¼ cups (300 ml) lukewarm water (110°–115°F/43°–46°C)

¾ cup plus 2 tablespoons (200 g) butter, at room temperature

Butter and jam, of choice for serving

Makes 24 small rolls

Sift together the flour and salt into a large bowl. In a small bowl, stir together the yeast, sugar, and 2 tablespoons of the lukewarm water and let stand until bubbles appear, about 2 minutes. Make a well in the center of the flour mixture and pour the yeast mixture and most of the remaining water into it. Using a wooden spoon, gradually draw the flour into the well and mix with the liquid to form a firm dough, adding the last of the water if the dough is too dry to hold together. Then, using your hands, knead the dough in the bowl until it is smooth, uniform, and springs back to the touch, about 5 minutes. Cover the bowl with a damp kitchen towel and leave in a warm place until the dough doubles in size, about 30 minutes.

Tip the dough out onto a floured work surface and knead for a few minutes until smooth and quite firm to the touch. Roll out into a rectangle about 8 by 12 inches (20 by 30 cm) and ⅓ inch (9 mm) thick. Cut the butter into small flakes. Scatter one-third of the butter evenly over the top two-thirds of the dough. Fold up the bottom one-third of the dough, then fold down the top one-third, seal the edges with a rolling pin, and refrigerate for 10 minutes. Repeat the entire process two more times, rotating the dough 90 degrees each time before rolling. Then repeat the process one more time without adding butter.

Roll out the dough into a rectangle 10 by 15 inches (25 by 38 cm) and ½ inch (12 mm) thick. Cut the dough into twenty-four 2½-inch (6-cm) squares. Bring two diagonally opposite corners to the center of each square and press together. Place the shaped butteries, joint side down, on a large sheet pan, spacing them about 2 inches (5 cm) apart. Let stand in a warm place for 30 minutes to rise. Preheat the oven to 400°F (200°C).

Bake the butteries for 10 minutes, then flip them over, lower the oven temperature to 350°F (180°C), and continue to bake until golden and crisp, 10–15 minutes longer. Transfer to a wire rack and let cool slightly before serving with butter and jam.

Highlanders

These buttery shortbread biscuits originated in the Scottish Highlands, hence their name. The dough is shaped into a log and rolled in demerara sugar before slicing and baking, which gives the biscuits a uniquely crunchy edge.

½ cup (115 g) butter,
at room temperature

¼ cup (50 g) superfine sugar

½ teaspoon pure vanilla extract

1⅓ cups (170 g) cake flour

3 tablespoons rice flour or
fine polenta

Demerara sugar, for rolling

Whole milk, for brushing

MAKES ABOUT 30 BISCUITS

In a bowl, using an electric mixer, beat together the butter and superfine sugar on medium speed until light and creamy. Add the vanilla and beat until well mixed. Add the flours and stir with a wooden spoon just until blended.

Tip the dough out onto a lightly floured work surface and shape it into a log about 2½ inches (6 cm) in diameter. Spread a thin layer of demerara sugar on a flat plate or sheet pan. Brush the dough log lightly on all sides with the milk, then roll the log in the Demerara sugar to coat evenly. Chill in the refrigerator for 20 minutes.

While the dough is chilling, preheat the oven to 425°F (220°C). Line 2 sheet pans with parchment paper or silicone mats.

Using a sharp, thin knife, cut the chilled dough into about 30 thin slices. Arrange the slices about 1 inch (2.5 cm) apart on the prepared pans. Bake the biscuits until lightly golden, 15–20 minutes. Let cool on the pans on wire racks for 5 minutes, then transfer to the racks and let cool completely. The biscuits will keep in an airtight container at room temperature for up to 4 days.

Selkirk Bannock

Named after the historic Scottish town of Selkirk, this small, rich, yeasted loaf, shaped like the round cob loaf, was known to be a favorite of Queen Victoria to accompany a cup of tea. Traditionally, it is packed with golden raisins (sultanas) and is made with half butter and half lard. In this recipe, dried cranberries and pecans replace the raisins, a little mixed spice is added, and only butter is used. Wonderful eaten fresh from the oven, slices of this fruit-laced loaf are equally delicious toasted a day or two later.

¾ cup plus 2 tablespoons (200 ml) whole milk

3 tablespoons active dry yeast

½ cup plus 2 tablespoons (125 g) Demerara sugar

½ cup (115 g) butter, at room temperature

4 cups (500 g) bread flour

1 teaspoon mixed spice (see Chef's Note, page 38)

Pinch of salt

¾ cup (100 g) unsweetened dried cranberries

½ cup (50 g) pecan halves, roughly chopped

FOR THE GLAZE

2 tablespoons whole milk

1 tablespoon superfine sugar

MAKES 2 LOAVES; SERVES 12

In a small saucepan, heat the milk to lukewarm (110°–115°F/ 43°–46°C). In a small bowl, stir together the yeast, 1 teaspoon of the Demerara sugar, and 2 tablespoons of the lukewarm milk and let stand until bubbles start to appear, about 2 minutes. While the yeast is proofing, add the butter to the milk in the saucepan and heat over low heat just until the butter melts, then remove from the heat and let cool to lukewarm.

Sift together the flour, mixed spice, and salt into a large bowl. Make a well in the center of the flour mixture and add the yeast mixture and most of the milk-butter mixture to the well. Using a wooden spoon, gradually draw the flour into the well and mix with the liquid ingredients to form a fairly soft dough, adding the last of the liquid if the dough is too dry to hold together. Turn the dough out onto a lightly floured work surface and, using your hands, knead the dough until it is smooth and springs back to the touch, at least 5 minutes. Return the dough to the bowl, cover the bowl with a damp kitchen towel, and leave in a warm place until the dough has doubled in size, about 30 minutes.

Tip the dough out onto a floured work surface. Pat it into a large oval and sprinkle evenly with the remaining Demerara sugar, the cranberries, and the nuts. Fold the dough over and knead it lightly to distribute the sugar, fruit, and nuts evenly. Cut the dough in half, then shape each half into a small round. Place the rounds on a sheet pan and leave to rise in a warm place for 20–30 minutes.

Recipe continues on the following page

Continued from the previous page

Meanwhile, preheat the oven to 425°F (220°C).

Using a sharp, thin knife, make a shallow cross in the top of each loaf. Bake the loaves for 15 minutes, then turn down the oven temperature to 350°F (180°C) and continue to bake until golden brown and the loaf sounds hollow when tapped on the base, 20–25 minutes.

While the loaves are baking, make the glaze. Heat the milk until hot, then remove from the heat and stir in the sugar until dissolved.

Remove the bannocks from the oven about 5 minutes before they are done and brush them liberally with the glaze, then return them to the oven to finish baking. Let cool on the pan on a wire rack for 5 minutes, then transfer to the rack and let cool for 5 minutes more before slicing and serving.

Flowers for Tea

Kew Palace, which sits in the grounds of Kew Gardens on the banks of the River Thames, is the smallest of all the royal palaces. It was built in 1631 atop a fifteenth-century undercroft (vaulted chamber) as a fashionable manor house for Samuel Fortrey, a successful London silk merchant, and was originally called the Dutch House. The construction is of distinctive red bricks laid in a style known as Flemish bond, in which alternating the sides and ends of bricks creates a pleasing, decorative pattern. The gabled front gives the house a Dutch appearance; some describe it as the look of a dollhouse.

In 1729, George II and Queen Caroline became the first royalty to take an interest in Kew, deciding it would be an ideal residence for their three eldest daughters, Anne, Caroline, and Amelia. After them, several generations of Georgian royalty used the palace and nearby Richmond Lodge as weekend refuges from the demands of royal life in the center of London. At the end of the nineteenth century, Queen Victoria ordered that it should be opened to the public, and about one hundred years later, it underwent extensive restoration. In 2006, Prince Charles hosted a dinner at the palace to celebrate the eightieth birthday of the Queen.

While the palace is little known, the surrounding Kew Gardens are world renowned, having one of the most diverse collections of living plants of any botanic garden in the world. Numerous specialist gardens exist within Kew as well. One of the most fascinating is the Kitchen Garden, where much research surrounding food sustainability is undertaken, a subject very close to Prince Charles's heart. Many heritage and rare varieties of fruits and vegetables are grown here, some of which were also grown in the kitchen garden at Highgrove. It was a joy to have access to produce that was so incredible, both in appearance and taste. To this day, I am inspired by the beauty of just-picked fruits, vegetables, and flowers. Edible flowers, in particular, make the most wonderful garnishes for savory dishes and the most stunning decoration for cakes and desserts. This chapter is devoted to a very pretty floral afternoon tea.

The Temperate House at Kew Gardens is the world's largest Victorian glasshouse.

Mini Vanilla, Ginger, and Buttermilk Loaves

*T*his is an amazing cake recipe; no one ever suspects that it is gluten-free. Served "naked" with a simple lemon glaze and no frosting, the cake speaks for itself. It is beautifully moist and the flavors of the vanilla, stem ginger, buttermilk, and lemon together are delectable.

FOR THE CAKE

1 cup (225 g) butter, at room temperature

1 cup plus 2 tablespoons (225 g) superfine sugar

4 free-range eggs

1½ cups (140 g) ground almonds

1 cup (125 g) all-purpose gluten-free flour blend

1 teaspoon gluten-free baking powder

Pinch of salt

½ teaspoon xanthan gum

3 tablespoons buttermilk

1 teaspoon pure vanilla extract

4 bulbs stem ginger in syrup, finely grated

1 tablespoon syrup from stem ginger

FOR THE GLAZE

1 cup plus 1 tablespoon (125 g) confectioners' sugar

¼ cup (60 ml) fresh lemon juice

1 tablespoon water

Finely grated zest of 1 lemon

FOR THE DECORATION

Edible small fresh flowers

Confectioners' sugar, for dusting

Makes 12 mini loaves

To make the cake, preheat the oven to 350°F (180°C). Line twelve 3 x 1¾-inch (8 x 4.5-cm) mini loaf pans with parchment paper. Place the pans on a large sheet pan.

In a large bowl, using a wooden spoon, mix together the butter and superfine sugar until light and creamy. Add the eggs, one at a time, beating well after each addition. If the mixture begins to curdle, whisk in a few spoons of the flour. Add the ground nuts, (remaining) flour, baking powder, salt, and xanthan gum and, using a rubber spatula, fold them in just until fully incorporated. Finally, stir in the buttermilk, vanilla, grated ginger, and ginger syrup until well blended.

Divide the batter evenly among the prepared pans. Bake the loaves until they are golden on top and spring back to the touch, 15–18 minutes. Let cool in the pans on a wire rack for a few minutes, then turn them out onto the rack and turn right side up. Set the rack over a sheet pan.

While the loaves are baking, make the glaze. In a small pan over medium heat, combine the confectioners' sugar, lemon juice, and water and heat, stirring, until a smooth, quite runny, translucent icing forms. Remove from the heat and stir in the lemon zest.

While the loaves are still warm, brush the glaze on the top and sides of each loaf, then let cool completely. Just before serving, top each loaf with flowers and a very light dusting of confectioners' sugar.

Chilled Lime Tartlets

These refreshing lime tartlets take only a matter of minutes to make. They are perfect for an alfresco summer afternoon tea.

Light vegetable oil, for the molds

FOR THE BASE

5 oz (140 g) shortbread biscuits

5 tablespoons (70 g) butter, melted and cooled

FOR THE FILLING

⅔ cup (150 ml) heavy cream

1 can (14 oz/397 g) sweetened condensed milk

3 limes

FOR THE DECORATION

8 small strawberries, preferably wild

8 small fresh mint sprigs

Fresh chamomile flowers or other small, edible seasonal blossoms

MAKES 8 TARTLETS

Line a large sheet pan with plastic wrap or a silicone mat. Oil the inside of eight 3-inch (7.5-cm) heart-shaped ring molds or eight 2½-inch (6-cm) round ring molds. Place the molds on the prepared pan.

To make the base, in a food processor, pulse the biscuits until they are reduced to fine crumbs. Add the butter and process briefly to moisten evenly. Divide the crumb mixture evenly among the prepared molds, pressing down on the mixture with the back of a spoon. Chill the molds in the refrigerator while making the filling.

To make the filling, in a bowl, using an electric mixer, beat the cream on low speed until thick. Using a spoon, fold the condensed milk into the cream. Finely grate the lime zest directly into the cream, then juice the limes and stir the juice and zest into the cream. The mixture will thicken. Spoon the filling into the molds, dividing it evenly, and smooth the tops. Chill the tartlets in the refrigerator for 2 hours to set the filling.

To serve, carefully lift away the rings from around the tartlets and place each tartlet on a plate. Decorate with the strawberries, mint, and flowers and serve chilled.

 CHEF'S NOTE

Graham crackers can be substituted for the shortbread biscuits and lemon can be used instead of lime.

"Bunch of Flowers" Biscuits

These delicious flower-shaped biscuits make a lovely centerpiece for a floral-themed afternoon tea. Present them in a jug or a vase, with or without some fresh green foliage, such as stems of rosemary, mint, sage, or thyme. The biscuit dough contains golden syrup (or honey), which makes it pliable enough for you to insert wooden skewers before baking without the dough crumbling. Decorating the biscuits is a great activity for children, especially when you have icing in a range of bright colors and plenty of sprinkles and sparkles!

7 tablespoons (85 g) superfine sugar

6 tablespoons (85 g) butter, at room temperature

¼ cup (85 g) golden syrup

1 free-range egg yolk

1 teaspoon pure vanilla extract

2½ cups (300 g) cake flour

½ teaspoon baking powder

Long, thin wooden skewers

FOR THE DECORATION

Selection of premade colored icings

Selection of sprinkles

MAKES 36 BISCUITS

In a large bowl, using an electric mixer, beat together the sugar, butter, golden syrup, egg yolk, and vanilla on low speed until well mixed and no lumps of butter remain, about 3 minutes. Sift together the flour and baking powder directly into the bowl. Continue to beat until the flour mixture is fully incorporated and a dough forms that clings together and has pulled away from the sides of the bowl. Gather up the dough into a ball, flatten into a disk, wrap in plastic wrap, and chill in the refrigerator for 20 minutes.

Line 2 sheet pans with parchment paper or silicone mats. Turn the dough out onto a lightly floured work surface and roll out ¼ inch (6 mm) thick. Using a 3-inch (7.5-cm) round or flower-shaped cutter, cut out as many biscuits as possible and transfer them to the prepared pans. Carefully insert a thin wooden skewer into each biscuit to create the "stem" of the flower, pushing it all the way to the center. Arrange the "flowers" well spaced on the sheet pans to allow for the skewers and for slight spreading during baking. Gather up the scraps, press together, reroll, cut out more biscuits, and add them to the pans. Chill in the refrigerator for 20 minutes. Meanwhile, preheat the oven to 300°F (150°C).

Bake the biscuits, rotating the pans back to front halfway through baking, until golden, 15–18 minutes. Let cool on the pans on wire racks for 10 minutes, then transfer to the racks and let cool completely.

Using the icings and sprinkles, decorate the cooled biscuits as desired.

CHEF'S NOTE

A few of these "flower" biscuits make a lovely gift when tied together with a ribbon and wrapped in eco-cellophane.

Rose and White Chocolate Cupcakes

*T*he perfect size for afternoon tea, these pretty, little cupcakes are especially welcome when there is a large selection on offer and you want to try a little of everything! The white buttercream is flavored with vanilla, while the pink has a splash of rose water in it.

FOR THE CUPCAKES

¾ cup (170 g) butter, at room temperature

¾ cup plus 2 tablespoons (175 g) superfine sugar

½ teaspoon pure vanilla extract

3 free-range eggs

1⅓ cups (175 g) cake flour

½ teaspoon baking powder

Pink natural food coloring, as needed

FOR THE BUTTERCREAM

3½ oz (100 g) white chocolate, chopped

7 tablespoons (100 g) butter, at room temperature

¾ cup plus 1½ teaspoons (100 g) confectioners' sugar, sifted

½ teaspoon pure vanilla extract

Few drops rose water

Pink natural food coloring, as needed

FOR THE DECORATION

Small roses or rose petals

Makes 24 mini or 12 large cupcakes

To make the cupcakes, preheat the oven to 350°F (180°C). Line 24 mini muffin cups or 12 standard muffin cups with paper liners.

In a large bowl, using an electric mixer, beat together the butter and sugar on medium speed until light and creamy. Beat in the vanilla and then add the eggs, one at a time, beating well after each addition. Sift together the flour and baking powder directly into the bowl. On low speed, mix just until incorporated. Starting with 1 or 2 drops, stir in just enough food coloring to create a delicate pink.

Spoon the batter into the prepared muffin cups, dividing it evenly. Bake the cupcakes until they spring back to the touch and a toothpick inserted into the center comes out clean, 10–12 minutes for the mini cupcakes and 18–20 minutes for the larger ones. Let cool in the pan on a wire rack for a few minutes, then transfer the cupcakes to the rack and let cool completely.

While the cupcakes are baking, make the buttercream. Put the chocolate into a small heatproof bowl over (not touching) barely simmering water in a saucepan and heat, stirring occasionally, until the chocolate melts and is smooth. Remove from over the heat and let cool completely.

In a bowl, using the electric mixer, beat the butter on low speed until creamy. Add the confectioners' sugar and continue beating until the mixture is very light and creamy. With the mixer running, gradually pour in the melted chocolate and continue beating until all the chocolate has been added and is well mixed.

Recipe continues on the following page

Continued from the previous page

Divide the buttercream evenly between 2 small bowls. Stir the vanilla into 1 bowl. Add the rose water and then the food coloring to the second bowl, starting with 1 or 2 drops of each and adding just enough to achieve a pleasant rose flavor and a pretty pink color. Spoon each batch of buttercream into a piping bag fitted with a ⅓-inch (9-mm) open star tip.

When the cupcakes are completely cool, pipe a swirl of buttercream onto the top of each one, then decorate with a small rose or some rose petals.

 CHEF'S NOTE

Use the rose water sparingly, as too much will make the buttercream taste soapy.

Windsor Castle

Special Wedding Afternoon Tea

Windsor Castle stands, proud and imposing, on a chalk bluff above the River Thames. It is the largest inhabited castle in the world and the longest-occupied castle in Europe. In 1070, William the Conqueror started building a defensive circle of fortresses around London; this was how Windsor Castle began. Over the centuries, it has been transformed into the stunning castle that it is today. When she is based in London, the Queen escapes to Windsor Castle for the weekends. She can ride and enjoy other outdoor pursuits in Windsor Great Park and Home Park.

I can attest to the vastness of the castle, as the first time that I worked there I frequently became disoriented. On one occasion, feeling thoroughly lost, I opened a door that revealed a beautiful drawing room, and a kindly voice asked, "Are you lost my dear?" It was Princess Margaret, the Queen's sister! She gave me directions and sent me on my way.

Banquets and state occasions are sometimes held at Windsor, though the majority of them are at Buckingham Palace. I was very fortunate to work on some wonderful events at Windsor, a location so splendid that the pressure to produce food of a spectacular nature is great! I also attended a Christmas dance at Windsor as a guest, and it certainly felt like a night out of a fairy tale.

St. George's Chapel at Windsor Castle has been a popular venue for royal weddings. Seventeen royal couples have married there, dating as far back as 1863, and in the past thirty years, six weddings have taken place in the chapel. Prince Charles and the Duchess of Cornwall were married there in 2005 and most recently Harry and Meghan. Looking back over all the royal wedding menus, it is fascinating to see how each one reflects the changing times. Prince Charles has greatly influenced the way many British people view the provenance of the food they eat. Wedding food has been greatly simplified over the years, and recently the emphasis has been on using locally sourced, seasonal, organic produce.

All the recipes in this chapter are inspired by the menus from the weddings of Prince Charles and Prince Harry. They reflect the simplicity of the food that was served, starting with an informal yet elegant wedding cake with fresh flowers that has replaced the rich, ornate traditional wedding cake covered in sugar craft.

Lemon and Elderflower Cake

Harry and Meghan had a lemon and elderflower wedding cake, but you don't have to wait for a wedding to make this! Light lemon sponge drizzled with an elderflower syrup is filled with lemon curd and a tangy lemon buttercream. If you don't want to have a tiered cake, you can make a regular layer cake, using two or three cake pans of the same size.

FOR THE CAKE

2 cups (450 g) butter, at room temperature, plus more for the cake pans

2½ cups (500 g) superfine sugar

10 free-range eggs

3 lemons

3⅔ cups (455 g) cake flour

5 teaspoons baking powder

6 tablespoons (75 g) plain Greek yogurt

FOR THE SYRUP

¼ cup (60 ml) elderflower cordial

1 tablespoon fresh lemon juice

3 tablespoons superfine sugar

FOR THE BUTTERCREAM

5½ tablespoons (80 g) butter, at room temperature

1⅔ cups (200 g) confectioners' sugar, sifted

3 tablespoons cream cheese, at room temperature

Finely grated zest of 1 lemon

1 tablespoon fresh lemon juice

Yellow natural food coloring, as needed

FOR THE FILLING AND DECORATION

1 cup (220 g) lemon curd

Elderflowers or other edible fresh yellow, cream, or white flowers

16 long fresh thyme sprigs

SERVES 18

To make the cake, preheat the oven to 350°F (180°C). Butter the sides of one 9-inch (23-cm), one 6-inch (15-cm), and one 3-inch (7.5-cm) round cake pan with 4-inch (10-cm) sides and line the bottom of each pan with parchment paper.

In a large bowl, using an electric mixer, beat together the butter and superfine sugar on medium speed until light and creamy. Break the eggs into a medium bowl and whisk lightly. On medium speed, gradually add the eggs to the butter mixture and beat until well mixed. If the mixture begins to curdle, beat in a few spoons of the flour. Grate the zest from the 3 lemons directly into the butter mixture. Then juice 2 of the lemons, add the lemon juice to the butter mixture, and beat on medium speed until the zest and juice are incorporated. Sift together the (remaining) flour and baking powder directly into the bowl. Using a large metal spoon or a rubber spatula, stir in the flour mixture just until fully incorporated, then stir in the yogurt, mixing well.

Divide the batter among the prepared cake pans, filling each pan to within 1 inch (2.5 cm) of the rim. Using an offset spatula, smooth the surface in each pan, then make a small hollow in the center so the top is flat when the cake layer emerges from the oven.

Bake the cake layers until the tops are golden and spring back to the touch and a toothpick inserted into the center comes out clean, 30–35 minutes for the largest layer, 20–25 minutes for the medium-size layer, and 10–12 minutes for the small layer. Let cool in the pans on wire racks for 5 minutes, then invert the pans onto the racks, lift off the pans, and turn the layers right side up.

Recipe continues on the following page

Continued from the previous page

Just as the cake layers have finished baking, make the syrup. In a small saucepan over medium heat, combine the elderflower cordial, lemon juice, and superfine sugar. Bring to a gentle boil, stirring to dissolve the sugar, then remove from the heat and let cool for a few minutes.

Once you have removed the cake layers from their pans, brush the warm syrup over the tops and sides of the warm layers, then let the layers cool completely.

To make the buttercream, in a bowl, using an electric mixer, beat the butter on high speed until very pale, light, and creamy. Add the confectioners' sugar and beat until combined, then add the cream cheese and beat until incorporated. Lastly, add the lemon zest and juice and just enough food coloring to create a pale lemon yellow. Beat on high speed until the buttercream is very smooth and light and evenly tinted.

To assemble and decorate the cake, using a long serrated knife, split each cake layer in half horizontally. Place the bottom half of the largest layer, cut side up, on a serving plate. Spread first with a generous layer of the buttercream and then with a layer of lemon curd, extending them to the edge of the layer. Top with the second half of the cake, cut side down, and cover the top and sides with the buttercream. Repeat to fill and ice the medium and small layers the same way, stacking the smaller cakes directly on top of each other in the center of the large one. Decorate the cake with the flowers of your choice and thyme sprigs.

Coffee and Hazelnut Macaroons

Macaroons of many flavors and colors have appeared on royal wedding menus throughout the ages. These are larger and more rustic than the classic French macarons, *and they are a lot simpler to make. They have a thin, crisp outer shell, a delightfully chewy center, and an indulgent chocolate ganache filling.*

FOR THE MACAROONS

¾ cup plus 1 tablespoon (115 g) skinned hazelnuts, toasted

1 cup (200 g) superfine sugar

1 tablespoon cornstarch

1 tablespoon dark-roast instant coffee powder

2 free-range egg whites

1 teaspoon pure vanilla extract

FOR THE CHOCOLATE GANACHE

4 oz (115 g) bittersweet chocolate, finely chopped

½ cup (120 ml) heavy cream

1 teaspoon pure vanilla extract

Confectioners' sugar, for dusting

MAKES 15 MACAROONS

To make the macaroons, preheat the oven to 350°F (180°C). Line 2 sheet pans with parchment paper or silicone mats.

In a food processor, combine the hazelnuts, half of the sugar, the cornstarch, and coffee powder and process until the nuts are finely ground. In a bowl, using an electric mixer, beat the egg whites on medium speed until they hold firm peaks. On medium speed, gradually add the remaining sugar, beating well after each addition. Continue beating on high speed until the meringue is thick and glossy. Using a metal spoon, fold the nut mixture and vanilla into the beaten egg whites just until evenly distributed.

Spoon the batter into a piping bag fitted with a ½-inch (12-mm) plain tip. Pipe 30 rounds, each 1½ inches (4 cm) in diameter, onto the prepared pans, spacing the rounds about 1 inch (2.5 cm) apart. Bake the macaroons until golden, 15–20 minutes. Let cool on the pans on wire racks for 5 minutes, then transfer to the racks and let cool completely.

To make the ganache, put the chocolate into a heatproof bowl. In a small saucepan over medium heat, bring the cream to a boil. Remove from the heat, pour the cream over the chocolate, and stir until the chocolate has melted. Leave to one side to cool completely, then beat the ganache with a rubber spatula until smooth.

Turn half of the macaroons bottom side up on a work surface. Spoon the ganache into a piping bag fitted with a ½-inch (12-mm) plain tip and pipe a ½-inch (12-mm) spot of ganache in the center and a line of ganache around the edge of each overturned macaroon. Top with a second macaroon, bottom side down, and gently press together.

Lightly dust the tops of the macaroons with confectioners' sugar before serving.

Rhubarb and White Chocolate Tartlets

*I*n this recipe, thin, crisp, golden filo pastry shells are filled with unctuous white chocolate–vanilla mousse and topped with tart rhubarb—a heavenly marriage of crunchy, creamy, and tangy. Harry and Meghan served rhubarb tartlets at their wedding, which recalled a little taste of Harry's childhood and the wonderful rhubarb grown at Highgrove.

4 rhubarb stalks

3 tablespoons water

¼ cup (50 g) superfine sugar

4 large sheets filo pastry, thawed according to package directions if frozen

Flour, for dusting

3 tablespoons butter, melted

FOR THE MOUSSE

10 ½ oz (300 g) white chocolate, chopped

1¼ cups (250 g) plain Greek yogurt

1 teaspoon pure vanilla extract

FOR THE DECORATION

12 raspberries

12 small white edible flowers, such as chamomile

MAKES 12 TARTLETS

Preheat the oven to 350°F (180°C). Place twelve 3-inch (7.5-cm) fluted round tartlet molds or a 12-cup standard muffin pan on a sheet pan.

To prepare the rhubarb, trim off both ends of each stalk. If the stalks seem fibrous, peel them. (Rhubarb at the height of the season is usually tender enough not to need peeling.) Cut the stalks on the diagonal into 1-inch (2.5-cm) lengths. The pieces will have a lozenge shape. Transfer the pieces to a baking dish just large enough to hold them in a single layer. Add the water to the dish and then sprinkle the sugar over the rhubarb. Cover the dish with aluminium foil.

Bake the rhubarb until tender when pierced with a fork, about 15 minutes. Remove from the oven, uncover, and let cool completely.

To make the tartlets, lay a filo sheet on a lightly floured work surface, keeping the other sheets covered with plastic wrap to prevent them from drying out. Lightly brush the entire sheet with some of the butter. Lay a second sheet on top, then lightly brush the top sheet with butter. Cut the layered sheets into six 5-inch (13-cm) squares. Line 6 of the tartlet molds with a filo square, pressing the filo down firmly onto the base. Trim the edges where necessary so the pastry does not extend above the rim. Repeat with the remaining 2 filo sheets to line the remaining 6 tartlet molds.

Bake the tartlet shells until golden, 10–12 minutes. Let cool completely on the pan on a wire rack, then carefully remove them from the molds.

Recipe continues on the following page

Continued from the previous page

To make the mousse, put the chocolate into a heatproof medium bowl over (not touching) barely simmering water in a saucepan and heat, stirring occasionally, until the chocolate melts and is smooth. (Alternatively, heat in a microwave.) Remove from over the heat and let cool. Using a balloon whisk, gradually whisk the yogurt into the chocolate. The mixture may initially curdle, but as you continue adding the yogurt, it will become smooth and thick. Whisk in the vanilla.

To finish, spoon the mousse into the tartlet shells, dividing it evenly. Drain the rhubarb well and arrange the pieces on the top of each tartlet, finishing with a raspberry and a flower. Serve within a couple of hours, as the pastry softens if left longer.

Mini Cornish Pasties

These were an obvious choice for the wedding menu for Prince Charles and the Duchess of Cornwall. They are the most iconic food from Cornwall (though some may argue that clotted cream is). Originally pasties, or oggies as they are known locally, were made as a "packed lunch" for the miners. Sometimes they had meat at one end and apple at the other—main course and dessert all in one! The miners would toss away the thick, wide pastry edges where the pasty was held while eating to avoid being poisoned by the tin or copper dust from their fingers. Traditionally, Cornish pasties are made from beef, onion, potato, and rutabaga enclosed in a simple shortcrust pastry. These mini pasties filled with new potatoes, green onions, cheese, and lots of fresh herbs are are a wonderful warm addition to a celebratory afternoon tea spread.

1 tablespoon butter,
at room temperature

1 tablespoon olive oil

1 cup (100 g) finely diced green
onions, white and green parts

¾ cup (100 g) peeled and finely
diced carrot

¾ cup (100 g) finely diced
new potato

2 fresh thyme sprigs

Salt and freshly ground
black pepper

1½ lb (680 g) ready-made
shortcrust pastry dough

Flour, for dusting

3½ oz (100 g) Cornish Yarg or sharp
(mature) Cheddar cheese, finely
diced (about ¾ cup)

1 tablespoon finely chopped fresh
flat-leaf parsley

1 teaspoon finely chopped
fresh marjoram

1 free-range egg, beaten,
for the glaze

MAKES 12 PASTIES

Preheat the oven to 350°F (180°C). Have ready a large sheet pan.

In a heavy saucepan over medium heat, melt the butter with the oil. Add the onions, carrot, potato, and thyme and season lightly with salt and pepper. Cover and cook for a few minutes to soften the vegetables. Spoon into a bowl and let cool completely, then discard the thyme sprigs.

Roll out the pastry on a lightly floured work surface about ⅛ inch (3 mm) thick. Using a 5-inch (13-cm) plain round cutter, cut out as many 5-inch (13-cm) rounds as possible. (If you don't have the correct-size cutter, use an overturned saucer or bowl as a template.) Gather up the dough scraps, press together, reroll, and cut out more rounds until you have 12.

Add the cheese, parsley, and marjoram to the cooled vegetables and stir to mix. Place about 1 tablespoon of the filling in the center of each pastry round. Lightly brush the edge of each round with water, then fold the rounds in half, and, using your fingers, crimp the edges to seal so the crimping runs long the top of the pasty. Transfer the pasties to the sheet pan and brush them with the egg to glaze.

Bake the pasties until golden, 15–18 minutes. Serve warm.

Asparagus Spears Wrapped in Prosciutto with Chive Cream Cheese

The traditional season for asparagus in England runs from St. George's Day (April 23) to Midsummer's Eve (June 21). It's not surprising that English asparagus wrapped in dry-cured Cumbrian ham, a specialty of far northwestern England, was served at Harry and Meghan's May wedding; there is nothing to beat British asparagus, and it is a favorite of the royal family. In this recipe, prosciutto (Parma ham)—a stand-in for the Cumbrian ham—wraps neatly around the asparagus spears, and the concealed chive cream cheese is a delicious surprise.

36 small asparagus spears

6 tablespoons (90 g) cream cheese, at room temperature

1 tablespoon finely chopped fresh chives

Pinch of paprika

6 slices prosciutto

Fresh chives and chive flowers, for garnish

MAKES 12 "BUNCHES"

Snap off the slightly tough, woody bottom of each asparagus spear. Then, using a vegetable peeler, peel the bottom 2 inches (5 cm) or so of each stalk.

Have ready a large bowl of ice-cold water. Fill a saucepan with salted water, bring to a boil, and add the asparagus. Cook until just tender, 1–2 minutes, depending on the size of the spears. Drain and immediately refresh in the iced water. Then drain again and pat dry with paper towels.

In a small bowl, mix together the cream cheese, chives, and paprika. Cut each slice of prosciutto in half crosswise, then fold each half lengthwise to a width of about 1½ inches (4 cm). Spread 1½ teaspoons of the seasoned cream cheese onto the folded ham, then gather together 3 asparagus spears and wrap the ham, cheese side in, around them, securing them in a small "bunch." Repeat with the remaining asparagus, prosciutto, and cheese mixture to create 12 "bunches" in all.

Arrange on a platter, garnish with chives and flowers, and serve right away.

Caernarfon Castle

Traditional Welsh Afternoon Tea

Widely recognized as one of the finest examples of medieval architecture, Caernarfon Castle stands on the banks of the River Seiont in the County of Gwynedd in northwest Wales. Anglicized as Caernarvon and dating from the late eleventh century, it was a motte-and-bailey castle until the 1280s, when Edward I ordered the current stone structure to be built in its place. Caernarfon was used for the investiture of the Prince of Wales for the first time in 1911 for Prince Edward (later Edward VIII) and again in 1969, when Prince Charles was invested. Prince Charles received the title, which is traditionally given to the eldest son of the reigning monarch of the United Kingdom, in 1958 via letters patent, but his formal investiture would not take place until more than a decade later. He is now the longest-serving holder of the title. When Prince Charles ascends to the throne in the future, possibly Prince William will be invested as the next Prince of Wales here.

Following the ceremony of Prince Charles's investiture, the royal party and guests returned to HMY *Britannia*, the royal yacht, where the chefs would have laid on a wonderful meal befitting of the occasion and no doubt showcasing some of the greatest culinary traditions of Wales. The recipes in this chapter also represent some of the best-known and most-popular Welsh dishes and ingredients.

As the Prince of Wales, Prince Charles visits Wales regularly. I accompanied him on several trips and enjoyed the challenges of cooking in a very old castle. We stayed at the thirteenth-century Powys Castle, about two hours from Caernarfon by car.

HMY Britannia, the royal yacht, at sea.

Little Cinnamon and Blueberry Welsh Cakes

*T*raditionally, Welsh cakes are cooked on an iron griddle and are made from flour, sugar, currants, lard, and nutmeg. Their texture is a cross between that of a pancake and a scone. In this recipe, the currants are replaced by dried blueberries and cinnamon stands in for the nutmeg. Fresh from the griddle, these cakes are crisp on the outside, soft and velvety in the center, and beautifully scented with cinnamon. All they need is a little farmhouse butter and perhaps an extra dusting of cinnamon sugar or a drizzle of honey. They make a tasty, warm addition to a winter afternoon tea, and one is never enough!

1¾ cups (225 g) cake flour

¼ cup plus 2 tablespoons (75 g) superfine sugar

½ teaspoon baking powder

½ teaspoon cinnamon

7 tablespoons (100 g) butter, cut into small cubes, plus more for the griddle and for serving

⅓ cup (50 g) dried blueberries

1 free-range egg, beaten

1 teaspoon pure vanilla extract

Splash of whole milk, if needed

MAKES 15 CAKES

Sift together the flour, sugar, baking powder, cinnamon, and salt into a bowl. Add the butter and, using your fingertips, rub the butter into the dry ingredients until the mixture resembles fine bread crumbs. Add the blueberries and mix with your fingertips until incorporated. Then add the egg and vanilla and, using a rubber spatula, mix until a soft dough forms, adding the milk if needed. The dough should be a little softer than shortcrust pastry.

Transfer the dough to a lightly floured work surface. Using your fingers, press lightly into a round about ½ inch (12 mm) thick. Using a 2-inch (5-cm) plain round cutter, cut out as many rounds as possible. Gather up the scraps, press together, press out again, and cut out more rounds. You should have 15 rounds.

Heat a griddle or large, heavy frying pan over medium heat and add a knob of butter. When the butter melts, add as many cakes as will fit in the pan without crowding and cook until deeply golden on the underside, about 3 minutes. Flip over and continue cooking until they are well puffed up, the underside is golden, and the sides no longer look wet, about 3 minutes longer. Transfer to a plate and keep warm. Repeat to cook the remaining rounds the same way, adding more butter to the griddle or pan as needed.

These mini cakes are best served still warm from the griddle, with butter on the side.

Welsh Rarebit

While this dish is usually eaten for lunch or for a light supper, there is no reason not to serve little fingers of Welsh rarebit for tea, especially on a cold, gloomy afternoon. Although there is no definitive evidence that it originated in Wales, it is at the least an honorary Welsh dish, and a very popular one at that. The unctuous molten extra-mature Cheddar, punctuated with the tang of mustard and the malty notes of the beer, make it utterly irresistible. Use a really good bakery bread. Chunky slices of either sourdough or a malted granary farmhouse loaf (see Chef's Note, page 99) make the best Welsh rarebit. The soft, buttery onions in this recipe add a particularly wonderful dimension to this delectable dish.

3 tablespoons butter

2 medium yellow onions, thinly sliced

1 heaping tablespoon flour

½ cup (120 ml) dark beer

⅓ cup (75 ml) whole milk

1 teaspoon whole-grain mustard

Freshly ground black pepper

5½ oz (150 g) extra-sharp (extra-mature) Cheddar cheese, coarsely grated

1 tablespoon finely chopped fresh chives

2 thick slices sourdough or malted granary bread

Fresh herb sprigs, such as sage and/or rosemary, for garnish

MAKES 8 FINGERS

In a saucepan over low heat, melt the butter. Add the onions and cook very slowly, stirring occasionally, until soft and translucent, about 15 minutes. Stir the flour into the onions and cook, stirring, for 1 minute. Gradually stir in the beer and then the milk and continue to cook, stirring, until a thick sauce forms, about 3 minutes. Stir in the mustard and season to taste with pepper. Lastly, add the cheese and chives and stir until melted. Remove from the heat and let cool for 15 minutes.

While the cheese mixture is cooling, preheat the broiler. Place the bread slices on a sheet pan, slide the pan under the broiler, and broil the bread, turning once, until lightly toasted on both sides.

Spoon the cooled cheese mixture onto the toast, dividing it evenly. Return the pan to the broiler and broil until the topping is golden and bubbling, 4–6 minutes.

Cut each bread slice into 4 fingers and serve right away. Garnish the plate with herb sprigs.

Bara Brith

Bara brith, which translates as "speckled bread," is a traditional yeasted Welsh loaf laced with plenty of tea-soaked currants. It has the texture of an enriched bread, rather than that of cake, so it is best eaten sliced and buttered and can also be toasted. Here, I have used baking powder instead of yeast and have replaced the customary currants with dried figs, as they give the loaf a lovely rich "toffee" flavor and a slightly nutty texture.

1½ cups (225 g) golden raisins (sultanas)

1½ cups (225 g) soft dried figs, diced

1 cup plus 1 tablespoon (225 g) firmly packed light brown sugar

1¼ cups (300 ml) hot strong black tea

3⅔ cups (450 g) cake flour

1 tablespoon baking powder

2 teaspoons mixed spice (see Chef's Note, page 38)

1 free-range egg, beaten

Butter, for serving

SERVES 8—10

In a large bowl, combine the raisins, figs, sugar, and tea, cover, and leave at room temperature overnight.

The next day, preheat the oven to 325°F (165°C). Line an 8½ x 4½ x 2½-inch (21.5 x 11.5 x 6-cm) loaf pan with parchment paper.

Add the flour, baking powder, mixed spice, and egg to the soaked fruit mixture and stir until all the ingredients are well blended.

Spoon the batter into the prepared pan and spread evenly. Bake the loaf until brown on top and a toothpick inserted into the center comes out clean, about 1½ hours. Let cool in the pan on a wire rack for 10 minutes, then turn out onto the rack, turn right side up, and let cool completely before serving, accompanied with butter.

Leek and Caerphilly Tartlets

*L*eeks have long been a national emblem of Wales, and to this day, the Welsh will "wear a leek in their cap" (or perhaps pinned to their lapel) on St. David's Day, their national day. According to one legend, this custom is owed to David, a descendant of Welsh royalty, having asked his soldiers to wear leeks on their hat in the battle against the Saxon invaders. Caerphilly, a traditional cheese with a lemony flavor and a moist, slightly crumbly texture, is the best known of all Welsh cheeses.

1 sheet all-butter puff pastry, about ¾ lb (340 g), thawed according to package directions if frozen

Flour, for dusting

1 medium potato, peeled and cut into ¼-inch (6-mm) dice

2 tablespoons butter

1 fresh thyme sprig

2 medium leeks, white and light green parts, finely diced

1¾ oz (50 g) Caerphilly cheese (see Chef's Note), diced

¼ cup (55 g) crème fraîche

Salt and freshly ground black pepper

1 free-range egg, beaten, for the glaze

2 tablespoons whole-grain mustard

MAKES 12 TARTLETS

CHEF'S NOTE

The best substitute for Caerphilly cheese is a sharp (mature) Cheddar.

Preheat the oven to 350°F (180°C).

Lay the pastry sheet on a lightly floured work surface and roll out ¼ inch (6 mm) thick. Cut out twelve 3-inch (7.5-cm) squares. Carefully transfer them to a large sheet pan, spacing them about 2 inches (5 cm) apart. Use the pastry trimmings to make 24 strips each ¼ inch (6 mm) wide and 4 inches (10 cm) long. Transfer the strips to a plate or small sheet pan. Chill all the pastry in the refrigerator while you make the topping.

In a small saucepan over high heat, combine the potato with salted water to cover, bring to a boil, and boil until tender, about 5 minutes. Drain well and set aside in a medium bowl. In a small sauté pan over medium heat, melt the butter with the thyme. Add the leeks and cook, stirring occasionally, until tender, about 5 minutes. Remove and discard the thyme, then tip the leeks into the bowl with the potato. Add the cheese and crème fraîche and mix together, then season to taste with salt and pepper.

Remove the pastry from the refrigerator. Paint each pastry square with the egg, then spread ½ teaspoon of the mustard on the center of each square. Pile the topping on the center of each square (about 1 heaping tablespoon per square). Using 2 pastry strips, make a diagonal cover the mound of topping, lightly pressing the ends of the strips to the edge of the square.

Bake the tartlets until the pastry has puffed and is golden, 15–18 minutes. Let cool on the pan on a wire rack for a few minutes, then serve warm.

Index

weldon**owen**

An imprint of Insight Editions

P.O. Box 3088
San Rafael, CA 94912
www.weldonowen.com

CEO Raoul Goff
VP Publisher Roger Shaw

Associate Publisher Amy Marr
Editorial Assistant Jourdan Plautz
VP Creative Chrissy Kwasnik
Art Director Allister Fein

Editorial Director Katie Killebrew
VP Manufacturing Alix Nicholaeff
Production Manager Sam Taylor

Photographer John Kernick
Food Stylist Carolyn Robb
Prop Stylist Stephanie Bateman Sweet
Prop Assistant Alice Kernick

Weldon Owen would also like to thank Rachel
Markowitz and Sharon Silva.

Printed in China
10 9 8 7 6 5 4 3 2

ISBN: 978-1-68188-824-8

Acknowledgments

Thank you to the brilliant team at Weldon
Owen, in particular Roger Shaw, Amy
Marr, Allister Fein, and Sharon Silva. John
Kernick, your photographs are beautiful.
Stephanie Bateman Sweet, your attention
to detail is amazing. Deirdre Reford, your
encouragement and support throughout
the process of writing the book and during
the photoshoot were brilliant. Bill Schwartz,
without your introduction to Weldon Owen
this book would not have happened. I am so
grateful to each one of you, thank you.

I will be forever indebted to TRH The
Prince and Princess of Wales and TRH
The Duke and Duchess of Gloucester for
the incredible experiences and treasured
memories that my thirteen years as a royal
chef afforded me.